APPLE

Reaktion's Botanical series is the first of its kind, integrating horticultural and botanical writing with a broader account of the cultural and social impact of trees, plants and flowers.

APPLE

Marcia Reiss

REAKTION BOOKS

Published by
REAKTION BOOKS LTD
33 Great Sutton Street
London EC1V 0DX, UK

www.reaktionbooks.co.uk

First published 2015

Printed and bound in China by 1010 Printing International Ltd

A catalogue record for this book is available from the British Library

ISBN 978 1 78023 340 6

Contents

Introduction: Backyard Apples

Three old apple trees, the survivors of an unknown orchard, still grow around my mid-nineteenth-century home in upstate New York. I don't know how old they are or what kind of apples they bear. Their history is as mysterious as their unpredictable apple production, bountiful one year and barren the next, yet full of fragrant blossoms each spring. During the occasional seasons of bounty, my husband and I pick bushels of apples from the two trees close to the house and peel and slice them, carefully carving around the occasional worm. Small and mostly misshapen, they pale in comparison to the shiny red orbs in supermarket bins, but they add a delicious tang to apple sauce and sweetened desserts. The third tree, a tall, solitary figure in the meadow across the road, has not been pruned for generations, and its broad, twiggy head becomes a cloud of white blooms each May. It is a milestone in our landscape and a welcome sign of renewal. One of its largest branches, thicker than a man's thigh, has split off the main trunk. Bent like an elbow with its broad forearm resting on the ground, it still lives and sends up new shoots and buds every spring. The meadow grasses grow around it, and by the end of summer when the apples appear, the thicket is so dense that only deer can taste the fruit.

This trio of trees is a remnant of apple history, a microcosm of the orchards that grew on nearly every New York and New England

opposite: An old apple tree near the author's home is a survivor of the orchards that grew on nearly every New York and New England farm in the 19th century.

7

farm in the nineteenth century. They are the distant descendants of European transplants introduced in the early years of colonial settlement. But their story is much older than the orchards of America or Europe, and the tale is still unfolding. Both meat and drink, apples have been a staple of the human diet for millennia. Eaten out of hand, baked into pies and tarts, boiled into sauce, butter and jelly, pressed for cider and juice, distilled into brandy, vinegar and wine, and dried for a long-term food supply, they have sustained, delighted and intoxicated people throughout the world. The pruned branches of the tree were also put to good use for the intricate parts of early machines, the cogs, wheels and shuttles. Small branches, aromatic long after cutting, were turned into spoons to stir apple sauce and churn butter.[1] From the time of Charlemagne to Johnny Appleseed, America's apple evangelist of the nineteenth century, planting apple trees was a requirement for new settlements. It not only provided food and wood, but also helped people to put down roots, investing in the future of their new towns.

Commercial cultivation has become a global enterprise, with America and China as the largest producers, yet small orchards still

An old sign at a Vermont apple orchard that has been operated by the same family for several generations.

Red Delicious apples, temptingly red and shiny,
nonetheless usually reach the market bland and mealy.

have fresh apples for sale at their own farms, as farmers nearly everywhere did centuries ago. I buy apples from several small orchards
within a short drive of our home, eagerly awaiting the start of each
autumn when the fruit snaps with taste. For years I avoided supermarket apples, particularly the omnipresent Red Delicious. Shaped
like fat teeth, they are not at all toothsome, usually too sweet and
cottony after months in cold storage. This staple of the school
cafeteria has come to represent everything that went wrong with
modern apple breeding. But I have seen apple cultivation change
within my own lifetime, from the mass production of a handful of
uniform varieties to the increasing appearance of apples with improved
taste and texture. Australia's Granny Smith, New Zealand's Gala,
Japan's Fuji, Minnesota's Honeycrisp and several other recent introductions – and especially the growing number of small orchards
reviving heirloom apples (those dating back at least 50 years and
still untouched by modern breeding) – are finally giving the Red
Delicious serious competition.

Yet supermarket choices are still limited, and shoppers face higher prices for the tastier apples. My market carries more than a dozen kinds of apple, plus a few organic alternatives – a better selection than the two or three standards of the 1960s, but nowhere near the thousands of varieties available before the apple became a corporate product. In the autumn, when trees in the nearby orchards are dotted red with apples, the supermarket also offers bags of the local fruit along with those that have travelled thousands of miles across the country and from other continents.

But finding a tasty, healthy apple is still a challenge. I was disheartened to read a supermarket sign from one major producer boasting that its latest variety had reached the top of the apple sweetness chart, the pinnacle known as 'supersweet'. Even apples, supposedly the healthy alternative to junk food, are part of America's unrelenting promotion of sugary food. And the push towards ever-sweeter apples has made a mockery of 'an apple a day keeps the doctor away', since

Golden Delicious, one of the world's most popular apples, has fewer nutrients than many other varieties, according to a U.S. study in 2003.

the sweetest apples often have the fewest nutrients.[2] More troubling is the apple's recurring place on the 'Dirty Dozen' list, the annual rating of supermarket fruits and vegetables with the greatest pesticide residues. It has been on the list, compiled by a U.S. environmental organization, for years, and in 2011 and 2012 reached the unenviable position of number one.[3]

Things are looking more hopeful, though, for those wishing to find a better apple – and in some unlikely places. Apple picking in country orchards has been a tradition for generations of city dwellers, but even the Big Apple is experiencing a new apple movement, one that harks back to an old appreciation for the fruit's diverse flavours and textures, without today's chemicals. In 1758 New York City sent the first shipment of its own commercially grown apples to Europe. Benjamin Franklin, a diplomat in London at the time, had asked for his favourite, the Newtown Pippin. The first commercial orchard in the colonies, now located in Queens, a borough of New York City, had raised the variety in about 1730 from a chance seedling, known as a pippin. It became New York's most famous apple, and was in demand in Europe and America throughout the next century. Queen Victoria loved its piney flavour so much that Parliament lifted the import duty on it until the First World War.[4] But as New York growers followed the trend towards producing uniformly red, cloyingly sweet apples, the tart, green-tinged Newtown Pippin disappeared from grocery shops and farm stalls alike. Today, young urban gardeners are planting Newtown Pippin saplings in New York's inner-city neighbourhoods and parks, reconnecting New Yorkers to their apple history.[5] The same is happening with other heirloom varieties in Los Angeles, San Francisco, Seattle, Portland, Boston and Detroit.

The newfound zeal for heirlooms (also known as heritage or antique plants) is not limited to apples. Gardeners, farmers and foodies in many parts of the world are planting old varieties of fruit and vegetables to savour their lost taste. Whether your desire is for

Auguste Renoir, *Still-life with Apples*, oil on canvas.
Apples are the most prevalent fruit in still-life painting.

freshly picked sweetcorn or vine-ripened tomatoes, supermarket produce can never compete with the taste and nutritional value of seasonal food from your local farm stall or garden. So why all the fuss about apples? Because apples have always represented more than something we eat. My neighbours have many theories about why our local apple trees do or don't yield fruit each year. Centuries ago, an apple tree that flowered and bore fruit at the same time was considered a bad omen.[6] Today's explanations for apple-tree aberrations range from global warming and the decline of honeybees to folk tales and superstition. Depending upon your frame of mind, apples or no apples on the tree in your back garden could be a sign of good or bad things to come.

It is no surprise that the apple is still caught in the web of superstition, for it has been planted deep in the myths, religion and art of nearly every culture. Good apples and bad apples abound in stories and images throughout history. The apple is an icon of beauty, desire and sin; of wholesome country harvests, healthful eating and hidden poison. It is the most literary fruit, a repeated symbol of the written word, and the most prevalent fruit in still-life paintings. It has become a symbol in its own right, recognized as readily as a brand of computers, mobile phones and music as it is on supermarket shelves. In *Apples* (1998), the author and journalist Frank Browning, who grew up raising apples with his father in their Kentucky orchard, describes the fruit's complex appeal as both 'ordinary and magical, as common as toast, as elusive as dreams'.[7]

An apple tree, more than a century old and still bearing fruit,
in the garden of Margaret Roach, Copake Falls, New York.

one

Out of the Wild:
An Ode and a Lament

In early 1862, as he lay dying of tuberculosis, Henry David Thoreau pulled together some of his voluminous notes about nature into a long essay about apples. It appeared in the *Atlantic Monthly* at the end of the year, six months after his death. The article, 'Wild Apples', is an ode to the apple's unique appeal throughout history.[1] And it is even more in touch with concerns about the environment today than it was when he wrote it as a naturalist in the midst of the Industrial Revolution. Best known for his earlier works *Civil Disobedience* (1849) and *Walden; or, Life in the Woods* (1854), his most famous book, Thoreau is nonetheless at his lyrical best in his heartfelt appreciation for the wild apple – and fearful of its foreshortened future. After a brief but keenly observant lifetime of walks through the woods and fields surrounding his New England home, he sees the apple as the embodiment of mankind's highest qualities.

> I know of no trees which have more difficulties to contend with, and which more sturdily resist their foes . . . Every wild-apple shrub excites our expectation thus, somewhat as every wild child. It is, perhaps, a prince in disguise. What a lesson to man!

To Thoreau, there was no such thing as a bad apple, at least not in its natural state: 'All wild apples are handsome. They cannot be too gnarly and crabbed and rusty to look at. The gnarliest will have some

15

redeeming traits even to the eye.' He even likes rotten and half-frozen ones fallen from the tree, the ones that give cider its tang. But he does not disparage the cultivated apple, which grows on 'the most civilized of trees. . . . It is as harmless as a dove, as beautiful as a rose, and as valuable as flocks and herds. . . . It may be considered a symbol of peace no less than the olive.'

The only bad apples are the 'tame and forgettable' ones, which even 150 years ago were favoured by business-minded growers because they were uniform in appearance and easier to ship. In contrasting the 'bow-arrow tang' of a wild apple to the oversweet fruit recently appearing in the markets of New England, he makes a prescient complaint about the 'imported half-ripe fruits of the torrid South', foreshadowing the mealy apples and cardboard-hard tomatoes that took over supermarket shelves in the mid-twentieth century. Thoreau identifies with the wild apple, with full awareness that neither he nor the apple is truly wild: 'Nevertheless, our wild apple is wild only like myself, perchance, who belong not to the aboriginal race here,

Tiny crab apples like these on a tree in autumn were the first apples in the New World.

but have strayed into the woods from the cultivated stock.' Like the apple brought to the American colonies by white settlers, Thoreau is of European stock. The Walden woods were a rather tame wilderness within walking distance of his home, which he visited several times, taking a break from a year's sojourn in his cabin retreat. A cultivated man himself, Thoreau is familiar with the apple's biological history: 'It has been longer cultivated than any other, and so is more humanized.' But he worries about its future: 'Who knows but, like the dog, it will at length be no longer traceable to its wild original.'

Thoreau's ode to the apple ultimately becomes a lament for its disappearing wildness. He longs for the pure taste of an apple grown from seed, not from the increasing numbers of grafted trees that he believed were diluting its essence and replacing the wild forests. 'The rows of grafted fruit will never tempt me to wander amid them', he cries. His lament, like that of a hunter-gatherer overtaken by agriculture, was a voice in the wilderness at a time of change, and his preference for apples 'sour enough to set a squirrel's teeth on edge and make a jay scream' was not to everyone's taste. In the nineteenth century nearly all wild apples were used for making cider, the fermented drink with an alcoholic kick known in Europe, not the sweet juice that it later became in the United States.

Today, we owe the pleasure of biting into a sweet, crisp apple to the work of generations of breeders and growers who have perfected the fruit from both seedlings and grafted trees. But, like Thoreau, we also have much to regret about the state of the apple. In his time, when railways were expanding throughout the country, apple growers were already changing from local farmers to large commercial nurseries. Refrigerated railway trucks started carrying fruit just ten years after Thoreau's death. The bigger producers were sacrificing the taste of unique varieties for cosmetically appealing cultivars that could keep their looks during longer periods of storage and more distant distribution. Thoreau's essay foreshadows the mass production and tasteless apples of today along with our desire to recover the natural, vibrant taste of the wild. Not fully appreciated in his day, he became a hero

A farmer spreading apples on a roof to dry in Virginia, 1935. Dried apples provided essential food for generations of rural families during long winters.

in the back-to-nature movement of the 1970s, and his views continue to resonate in today's resurgence of heirloom apples.

But the apples we love have not been natural for centuries. Their story is a complex one. It ranges from the grafting techniques perfected by the Romans to the controlled-atmosphere warehouses of today's commercial producers and the latest genetic advances that offer both promising and ominous developments for the future. Apples have been caught up in the politics of patriotism and pesticides and even in the throes of capitalism and communism, all of which have shaped the way they have been grown across the globe. In the end, Thoreau may have been right about the long-lasting benefits of the wild apple, even though he never knew about its origins in the mountain forests of Central Asia. Discovered in Kazakhstan in the twentieth century, these ancient ancestors of today's apples hold the secret of the fruit's biodiversity and its survival in the future.

two

A Rose is a Rose is a Rose . . . is an Apple

G ertrude Stein was not thinking of apples when she wrote that famous line about the rose (from 'Sacred Emily', 1913), but the two are botanically linked. They both belong to the family Rosaceae. Like old-fashioned roses and with a sweet fragrance, apple blossoms are clear evidence of the close family connection. And the fruit of the rose, its red hips, resembles small apples. Robert Frost, perhaps thinking of Stein's phrase, made the botanical connection in his light-hearted poem 'The Rose Family' (*West-running Brook*, 1928): 'The theory now goes that the apple's a rose.' And he was right. As Frank Browning explains, the apple was 'the unlikely bastard child of an extra-conjugal affair between a primitive plum from the rose family and a wayward flower with white and yellow blossoms of the Spiraea family called meadowsweet'; the offspring were 'crude apples . . . as tiny and bitter as rose hips'.[1]

Of all the many members of the rose family, including most of the fruits we eat today – apples, pears, plums, quinces, peaches, cherries and several kinds of berry – the apple became 'the hardiest, most resilient and most diverse fruit on the earth'.[2] In common with most flowers, apple blossoms have male and female parts, but most trees cannot produce fruit on their own. Like humans, they need to mate with a partner to produce offspring. Some varieties, known as triploids, do not produce pollen, putting all their energy into producing large quantities of fruit. They depend on nearby trees to provide pollen for fertilization. Whatever the variety, all apple trees depend

421. Pirus Malus L. **Apfel.**

largely on bees to act as matchmakers, spreading pollen from the male stamens of a blossom on one tree to the female stigma of a blossom on another. Commercial breeders and researchers imitate the bees by removing the pollen from one tree and delicately placing it on the blossom of another, then covering the match to prevent further pollination. After the fruits develop, they plant the seeds and wait years to track the results of these 'arranged marriages'. A brave new world of apple breeding opened once the apple's genome was sequenced in 2010. By analysing the DNA of prospective apple mates, breeders can now predict the results of their matchmaking much faster and more accurately than they could previously. Before the age of modern hybridization, most apple varieties, according to the writer and gardener Roger Yepsen, were 'love children, the products of chance pollination between unknown parents'.[3]

As soon as the ancients started to eat apples, they began to give them a babel of names. However, the words for apple in pre-Roman

Crab apples in an etching of *c.* 1910.
opposite: *Malus pumila* 'Miller' in a botanical print of 1885. Roses and apples are members of the same botanical family, Rosaceae.

Pomona, Roman goddess of fruit trees, is shown cradling apples in her skirt in this tapestry panel, *c.* 1900, by Edward Burne-Jones. Her name comes from the Latin word for fruit, *pomum.*

European languages – the Germanic *aplu*, Celtic *abhall*, Welsh *avall* and Gaulic *afall* are remarkably similar to the modern English word.[4] Although it is not clear which came first, the crab apple or the Old English *crabbe* meaning bitter or sharp, the connection is clear between the sour taste of the crab apple and a crabby grouch. The Greek and Latin names for apple have more positive implications. 'The apple was early so important, and generally distributed,' Thoreau maintained, 'that its name traced to its root in many languages signifies fruit in general.'[5] The Greeks called it *melon*, a word that also meant riches. The Romans had two words for it, *pomum* and, more commonly, *malus*, the Latin word that became the taxonomic name for the genus that includes about two dozen species of apple. These include crab apples, generally used for cider, and sweet apples, the kind we enjoy both fresh and cooked. Some botanists insist on *Malus pumila* as the only correct species name for sweet apples, but they are more commonly known as *Malus domestica*, the name that will be used in this book. It includes some 9,000 varieties known today, both chance seedlings and high-tech hybrids, as familiar as Red Delicious, McIntosh and Granny Smith, first propagated in the nineteenth century, and as new as Snapdragon, RubyFrost and Kanzi, introduced to the market in 2013. While only a tiny fraction are on supermarket shelves, the thousands of cultivated varieties are testimony to the apple's great appeal and its extraordinary ability to reproduce itself in ever-changing ways.

Apples are the most widely distributed fruits on the planet, spread by man, beast, bird and bug over millions of years. Everything about the apple – its botanical make-up and growth patterns – enabled it to move and multiply, always changing its characteristics, even before it received any help from man. The promiscuous cross-breeding facilitated by pollinating bees created infinite genetic potential in every wild apple seed. Contrary to the adage 'the apple doesn't fall far from the tree', each apple seed, also known as a pip or a kernel, possesses an amazingly diverse set of genes that produces endless variations, always different from the parent tree. The apple genome, the complete set of DNA in each of its cells, has about 57,000 genes, more than the

A waxwing feeding on crab apples. Birds dropping apple seeds
have helped wild forests sprout up over wide areas.

genome of any other plant studied to date, and twice as many as that
of humans.[6] Pollination between different varieties does not change
the type of fruit on the parent trees, but the resulting seeds produce
new trees, often with radically different offspring. Trees grown from
the seed of a sweet apple can produce fruit that is disappointingly
hard and bracingly bitter, known as 'spitters' – just one bite is sour
enough to spit out – and more like the wild apples from which they
are descended. Or they can be sweeter than their parents, refreshingly
tart, or with a myriad flavours, like wine. Their skin can be red, yellow,
green or a combination of these colours, as well as smooth or rough
(known as russets). Apples are also an exception to the phrase 'more
than skin deep'. Often peeled and discarded, the skin is the main source
of the fruit's flavour and floral aroma, and of many of its nutrients.[7]

Cold Comfort

Apple seeds are fussy about their requirements for germination. Since the fruit is native to the temperate parts of the world, its seeds need cold to germinate, a fact that seems to disprove its origin in the Garden of Eden, or at least in its supposed location in Palestine – the climate there was simply too hot.[8] The seeds sprout only after sustained periods of cold, generally 60 or more days at 2°C (36°F), the winter climate of the areas where the fruit first took hold, Central Asia and North America. Apple trees must also have a period of cold before they can produce fruit. In 'Goodbye and Keep Cold' (*Harpers* magazine, 1920), Robert Frost reminds his orchard about this, speaking like a parent to a child, but reversing the usual warning to keep warm:

> No orchard's the worse for the wintriest storm;
> But one thing about it, it mustn't get warm.
> 'How often already you've had to be told,
> Keep cold, young orchard. Goodbye and keep cold.'

Once the temperature starts to fall below 7°C (45°F) in late autumn or early winter, the trees lose their leaves, reduce their rate of respiration and enter a dormant period. It is a time of invisible replenishment, as the roots silently draw up minerals from the soil. The low temperatures of late winter are also critical, providing a shock of cold that cracks the tightly sealed buds formed the previous summer. In warmer climates, chemicals are sometimes used to induce the buds to open. But once they have opened, a spring frost can kill the blossoms before they turn into fruit, leading orchardists in northern climates to take extreme steps. The forecast of a post-blossom frost has led some growers to hire helicopters to fly over the vulnerable trees at night, swooshing the frigid air up and away from the orchard. Spring frosts can be devastating to harvests one year, but are often followed by abundant crops the next. Producing fewer apples gives the trees a period of rest, the Vermont heirloom orchardist Ezekiel Goodband explains: 'The next year they act like they just came back from vacation.'[9]

Like Cézanne, you may prefer to place apples in a bowl on your table. It makes for an artful arrangement, but the best place to keep them is actually in your refrigerator, where the cold slows down their predestined journey to overripeness and rot. Refrigerated apples, especially those kept in high-humidity bins, can last ten times longer than those at room temperature.[10] Long before the invention of artificial refrigeration, it was cold storage that allowed apples to survive long voyages in the holds of ships or long winters in the loft of a barn, a frost-free cellar or an unheated room in a farmhouse. Some farmers sealed them in barrels and submerged them beneath the ice of a frozen stream, from which they emerged cold but still crisp in the spring.[11] Cold delays the production of a naturally occurring plant hormone known as ethylene. As apples and many other fruits ripen, they give off increasing amounts of ethylene as a gas, and this is what causes fruits and vegetables stored together to spoil, particularly apples. Bananas are especially sensitive to ethylene and should be kept at a distance from apples. The well-known phrase 'one bad apple spoils the whole barrel' was born of experience. Nineteenth-century apple growers may not have understood that bruised apples give off even more ethylene than in the normal ripening process, but they took pains to prevent their apples from jostling during shipment by cradling them in layers of straw inside the barrels, and carrying the barrels carefully. According to Eric Sloane (1905–1985), author of many books about American cultural history and folklore, 'the man who was caught rolling a barrel of apples lost his job at once.' Sloane cites an old almanac that warned: 'Watch a man gather apples and you will see either a careful man or a careless man.'[12]

Today, apples also receive great care in shipping, each one cradled in a cell of a cardboard honeycomb. But more sophisticated methods are used long before they reach their destinations. Cold storage puts apples into hibernation, slowing their respiration, which is the process of absorbing carbon dioxide, giving off oxygen and producing ethylene.

Soon after the Second World War, British scientists began to experiment with ways to stop the process altogether. By introducing nitrogen to displace the oxygen and carbon dioxide, they were able to put apples into a kind of suspended animation. The technique was perfected in the development of controlled-atmosphere (CA) warehouses, which are now used by most big producers. The fruit is picked before it fully ripens and stored in the CA warehouses; just before shipping, the amount of nitrogen is reduced or the apples are removed from the warehouses, allowing them to resume respiration and ripening. Some producers exporting apples over great distances, for example from New Zealand to the U.S. and UK, use mobile CA warehouses on board ships. The timing is tricky, however, because different kinds of apple ripen at different rates.

In 2007 a chemical, methylcyclopropene (given the more appealing name Smartfresh), was developed to inhibit the production of ethylene in fruit and vegetables.[13] Like CA storage, it can ensure a year-round supply of apples that would normally ripen only in the summer and autumn. The apples retain their youthful firmness and most of their nutrients, but lose some of their flavour. And, depending on how long they have spent in storage and how far they have travelled, the apples in your supermarket might not have long to go before they lose all their flavour and texture, even in your own refrigerator. If you pick your own apples at home or at a local orchard, those that ripen early, such as McIntosh, will last a few weeks in the refrigerator. Those that ripen in late autumn, such as Northern Spy, can last a few months.[14]

But, like everything else about the ever-changing apple, some trees have proved to be the exception to the rule. While all apples benefit from cold storage after picking, a few varieties have learned to produce fruit without an extended period of cold weather. Known as low-chill varieties, they have survived through selective breeding and have led to apples being produced in the mild winters of places like Southern California, where varieties such as Beverly Hills and Tropical Beauty are grown.[15] They are also thriving in other parts of

A Palestinian boy selling candy apples on the beach in Gaza City, 2011.
Selected breeding of varieties that do not require cold temperatures
has allowed apples to be grown in warm climates.

the world that were once thought too hot for apples, including the
lands of the Bible. Israel grows apples in the northern hills of Galilee,
and has developed a low-chill variety, Anna, which grows in the south.

Cultivated Crunch

An ageing apple follows an inevitable path from crisp to cottony, a
change that takes place within the fruit's cell structure. Widely spaced
and filled with air, the cells soften as the apple ages. When you bite
into an overripe apple, your teeth simply push the cells apart instead
of breaking them and releasing their pent-up juices.[16] An apple that
keeps its crunch is a winner in today's market. That quality made
Honeycrisp (known in Europe as Honeycrunch) famous after it was
introduced in 1991 – so much so that in 2006 it was selected as one
of the 'top 25 innovations that changed the world', a list that included
the development of Google.[17] Compiled by the Association of

University Technology Managers, the list was made up of discoveries derived from university research in the U.S. and Canada.

Honeycrisp was developed at the University of Minnesota, in a state that had been thought too cold to become a major apple producer. But after years of trial and error, the university researchers discovered that the state's short growing season had created something unique, not only in Minnesota but also in the commercial apple business – a fruit with outstanding flavour, crispness and juiciness that keeps these qualities for months in storage. By 2006, the variety had become so popular that it was commanding a premium and yielding desperately needed revenue for ailing orchards in Minnesota and other parts of the northern Midwest. It was also generating funds for the university, which owned the patent and was selling millions of Honeycrisp trees. The patent for this moneymaker expired in 2008, allowing growers throughout the world to cultivate it without paying franchise fees.

Honeycrisp apple.

29

In the meantime, the researchers had been busy developing other ways to capitalize on the success of Honeycrisp. In 2010 they released a hybrid, SweeTango, which combined Honeycrisp with their new flavourful variety Zestar to produce an even bigger crunch. Like its parents, the hybrid has the physical qualities that guarantee a juicy crunch: larger-than-average cells held together by a strong 'glue' that prevents them from sliding apart under pressure.[18] When you bite into a perfectly ripe SweeTango, your teeth burst the big cells and release a flood of juice into your mouth. The process produces a cracking sound, yielding a taste, according to John Seabrook of the *New Yorker*, that is 'a matter of acoustics . . . like hearing with your mouth, or tasting music'.[19] Another writer describes the sound of the crunch as 'like a board-breaking karate chop'.[20] Apple crunchiness is so important that a new computerized tool – a penetrometer – was developed in 2011 to determine crispness with great accuracy.[21] The old-fashioned alternative is blind testing by a panel of experts who taste many varieties, apple after apple, and record their sensory reactions. The downside can be apple fatigue and dulled senses. The new penetrometer is also blind to size and colour, but never tires of biting into apples and spitting out measurable results.

Core Principles

Before they sprout, apple seeds like to be on their own, free of the swaddling flesh of the intact fruit. The man celebrated for planting apple orchards on the American frontier, John Chapman (1774–1845), better known as Johnny Appleseed, may have learned this through practical experience. Poets, songwriters and novelists sang his praises, yet not many were specific about his methods. An exception was a popular children's poem of the late nineteenth century, 'Appleseed John' by a popular writer of the day, Lydia Maria Child. The poem describes the way he supposedly planted apple trees. The publication date is uncertain, but the poem was already in circulation in the year of Child's death, and it may have set many a child off on the wrong garden path:

> He took ripe apples in pay for chores,
> And carefully cut from them all the cores.
> He filled a bag full then wandered away,
> And no man saw him for many a day . . .
> With pointed cane deep holes he would bore,
> And in every hole he placed a core;
> Then covered them well, and left them there
> In keeping of sunshine, rain and air . . .[22]

The planting of apple cores undoubtedly appealed to Child's waste-not-want-not mentality. She was the author of a best-selling book, *The American Frugal Housewife* (1829), and, like Chapman, turned away from the increasing materialism of the era's rising middle class.[23] However well meaning, her poem is at odds with the apple seed's essential requirement for reproduction, separation from the core. The misapprehension persists even today. It is comforting to think that by throwing an apple core out of the car window, you are planting a new apple tree, rather than littering the side of the roadway. But before you congratulate yourself, consider the botanical facts. The part of the apple that we eat is a fleshy womb of tissue enveloping the seeds, and the core is a kind of placenta. Unlike the human womb, however, the apple core contains substances that inhibit germination.[24] An apple seed has its best chance of germinating when it is free of the core – a fact that Chapman probably discovered out of necessity. He collected seeds from the cheapest and most available source, not apple cores but pomace, the seed-rich residue from cider mills, a truly frugal way to spread apples throughout the land. Available free, pomace (from the Latin *pomum*, apple) offered an unlimited supply of seeds to anyone willing to collect the sticky stuff. Encased in pressed fruit, the seeds stayed moist as Chapman carried them in leather pouches on horseback or shovelled piles of pomace into canoes for trips along frontier rivers. Any pomace clinging to the seeds also provided fertilizer after planting. Chapman could not have covered as much ground as he did – thousands of acres – planting apples core by core.

Apple seeds contain cyanide, although not enough to kill you after eating a few. The poison has a practical purpose. The bitter taste encourages anyone eating the seeds to spit them out, and the cyanide also provides a key chemical function in the tree's growth. It bonds to other enzymes, enabling the trees to adapt to a wide range of soil and climate conditions.[25] Fortunately for the apple, animals are not as fastidious as humans in eating the fruit. In places where apples grow, nearly every wild creature that eats, eats apples: bears, deer, turkeys, beavers, rabbits, raccoons, squirrels, skunks and many others.[26] Most are happy to eat the fruit along with the core and seeds. Once your apple core lands by the side of the road, its future is most assured if an animal comes along and chews it up, ultimately depositing the intact seeds in a fertile pile of manure. The hard-coated seeds can survive the gastric acids in the animal's gut. Dung beetles also do their part in tunnelling through the manure pile and, in the process, burying the seeds. In prehistoric times, bears and wild horses played a particularly important role in distributing the bigger, sweeter apples. Small apples have been discovered intact in bear

A fieldfare (a species of thrush) eating a windfall apple in the snow. Nearly every wild creature that eats, eats apples.

faeces, indicating that the bears swallowed them whole, keeping the seeds locked within the apple. The larger, sweeter fruits, chewed with relish by bears and horses over thousands of years, eventually travelled from primordial forests to civilization.[27]

'To everything there is a season', the Bible tells us (Ecclesiastes 3:1), but the apple has more than one. Different varieties ripen at different times – early summer, midsummer and autumn – making them widely available for distribution. Given the right conditions, apple seeds will sprout and grow just about anywhere, a trait that Henry Thoreau saw as a noble characteristic: 'Most fruits which we prize and use depend entirely on our care. Corn and grain, potatoes, peaches, melons, etc. depend altogether on our planting; but the apple emulates man's independence and enterprise.'[28] Their adaptability and genetic individuality are a huge advantage for plant diversity. But for apple growers, they present a huge disadvantage, that of unpredictability. When a tree with large, sweet fruit yields offspring with small, bitter apples, the grower loses years of time and money. The way to eliminate the risk and ensure consistent fruit quality is to employ a technique that has been practised for thousands of years: grafting.

Carefree Sex

Grafting allows apple trees to keep producing fruit after pollination, but without the worry of unpredictable seeds. The technique simply joins parts of two established trees, selected for the specific characteristics that the grower wants to duplicate. One part comes from the roots and the other, known as the scion, is a small branch with unopened leaf buds from another variety. While the rootstock will determine some of the grafted tree's traits, particularly its height, the scion will control its fruit. The scion is inserted into the decapitated trunk of the rootstock, a little wax is applied and, if the graft takes, the cambium, the tissue between the bark and the wood, forms a vascular connection, allowing the scion to grow into a new tree that will bear apples of the same taste, colour and size. Plum and peach trees can share each other's rootstocks, but apples prefer their own kind, bonding only to apple rootstocks.[29] Heirloom orchardists and domestic gardeners gather scions with dormant buds in winter and store them in plastic bags in their refrigerators. Agricultural research centres that bank genetically diverse scions for the distant future store them in liquid nitrogen at -184°C (-300°F).[30]

Although Thoreau complained of the increasing number of grafted orchards in nineteenth-century New England, the technique had been practised by ancient civilizations on many different types of plant. The idea may have come from early agricultural workers observing natural grafts that occasionally occur between adjacent plants of the same species. The Chinese used the technique thousands of years ago on mulberry plants to create the best homes for silkworms. Ancient Syrians grafted grapevines 3,800 years ago, and archaeological evidence shows that this was an established way of propagating fruit trees 2,000 years ago in Babylonia.[31] The Romans established extensive orchards of grafted fruit trees, as detailed in the writings of their horticulturists. Their methods 'were developed to such a level of sophistication', according to the botanists Barrie E. Juniper and David J. Mabberley,

> that there is little that a modern-day horticulturist could have taught the first century Columella, author of *De Re Rustica*, or Pliny the Elder on even the finer points of grafting, budding, dwarfing rootstocks, and other techniques.[32]

Less is More

Today's apple orchards are not the stately rows of tall trees that once graced the landscape. A century ago, apple pickers had to scale trees 7.6–9 m (25–30 ft) tall. Ladders are rarely needed for the dwarf and semi-dwarf trees that make up today's commercial orchards and home gardens. They reach no higher than 3 m (10 ft), and some are less

Apple pickers, Brockport, New York, c. early 1900s. Tall trees were common in
U.S. apple orchards a century ago, but have been largely replaced by dwarf trees.

than half as tall. More like shrubs than trees, these shallow-rooted specimens need stakes and trellises to remain upright when their branches are heavy with fruit. But the new dwarfs are irresistible to growers. They can produce twice the yield of the old standards, and five or six times as many, or more, can be planted in the same space.

'If you asked an apple tree what it would like to do,' Ezekiel Goodband explains, 'it would produce apples every other year.'[33] Orchardists keep the trees producing annually by pruning them every year before the growing season begins, as Goodband does with the 5,000 trees in his orchard in Vermont, starting in November. Pruning triggers the tree's survival instinct and focuses its energy on production. Threatened by losing some of its branches, but determined to spread its seeds, it will then produce an abundance of small apples. Orchardists thin these out, forcing the trees to produce bigger apples. In some orchards, the trees are pruned into tall, narrow spindles, exposing the fruit to more sunlight and producing more uniformly red apples.

Smaller trees are also easier to prune, thin and harvest. Available in many pick-your-own apple orchards today, pedestrian-accessible trees are also the result of grafting, but the practice is hardly new. The progenitors of today's dwarf apple trees were discovered about 2,300 years ago by two famous students of Aristotle, Alexander and Theophrastus. Alexander found a low-growing apple tree on an expedition to Asia and sent it back to the Lyceum in Athens. Theophrastus described it in one of his comprehensive treatises on plants, noting that the variety had probably been grown for many years in Asia Minor. It was cultivated for centuries afterwards in Greece and Rome and in the monastery gardens and parterres of palaces and grand estates throughout Europe. In the fifteenth century, these miniatures were called Paradise apple trees. Two centuries later, on the cover of John Parkinson's comprehensive botanical treatise *Paradisi in Sole Paradisus* (1629), Adam is shown cutting a branch from a small apple tree. The illustration, which shows the branch in full leaf rather than with dormant buds, is far from realistic, but Parkinson apparently wanted to show the preferred method of cultivation.[34]

Risky Business

In an illustration of the famous line 'It's better to burn out than to fade away' from Neil Young's rock anthem 'Hey Hey, My My' (1979), dwarf apple trees wear out after relatively short lives of intensive fruit production. It takes patience to grow apples from seed, but a tree can far outlive the person who planted it, for as long as two or three centuries. The dwarf and semi-dwarf varieties bear fruit much sooner after planting than standard trees do, but the smaller ones have much shorter lives. And for all their advantages in producing consistent, predictable crops, grafted trees in large, commercial orchards are facing unpredictable risks. Grafting creates sterile clones, which cannot reproduce. More importantly, clones, like the ones in science-fiction tales, have a fatal flaw: they are more susceptible than seedlings to disease and debilitation.

As the use of dwarfing rootstocks increased in the nineteenth century, they proved to be particularly vulnerable to viruses that spread pathogens into the grafted trees. A cure was discovered in the early twentieth century at the East Malling Research Station in England. The treatment, a sophisticated form of tissue culture, led to hardier rootstocks. The programme was so successful that about 80 per cent of apple trees throughout the world are grafted on to East Malling-derived rootstocks.[35] But each new generation of cloned trees faces continuing threats. Apple trees are the target of a bombardment of attacks by insects, fungi, bacteria and viruses throughout the growing season. More than 500 kinds of insect – codling moths, canker worms, weevils, mites, aphids and other voracious pests – feast on the leaves, the source of the tree's energy. Since it takes the energy generated by 50 leaves to produce a single apple, every leaf serves a purpose. Further damage inflicted by invisible microorganisms – scab, fire blight, powdery mildew and other destructive diseases – can turn an innocent apple tree into a botanical Job.

Many of these threats have traditionally been kept under control by the natural selection of wild trees that led to stronger, more resistant seedlings. The development of large commercial orchards, however, has changed the resilient wild stock into relative weaklings. Their first disadvantage is living in big orchards. Planting rows of trees side by side is a time-honoured and convenient way to grow apple trees, yet it is inherently unnatural and risky for the trees. As in a crowded classroom during flu season, it is easy in big orchards of closely planted trees for bugs of all kinds to jump from tree to tree. During the rise of commercial apple growing in the nineteenth century, but before the widespread use of chemical insecticides and fungicides, insect infestation and disease became overwhelming problems. As the early twentieth-century botanist S. A. Beach explained, it nearly destroyed the growing apple industry in New York State, which had become the largest producer of apples in the country.

Because of these and other difficulties which faced them some orchardists eventually became so discouraged at the

Pruned McIntosh apple trees, Millerton, New York, 2013.

outlook that in the decade from 1880 to 1890 they began to cut down their commercial apple orchards.[36]

Chemicals soon came to the rescue, and by 1905 Beach proudly reported that 'on the whole the industry of growing apples rests now on a more stable and satisfactory basis than at any previous period in its history.'[37] He could not have foreseen the greater dangers that new breeding practices would bring. Although chemicals have kept the orchards growing ever larger, most of the apples produced commercially today are clones of just a handful of varieties, those with the looks and taste that have made them market superstars. The clones are as sweet and beautiful as their parents, but, grafted over and over again from the same varieties, they have a drastically reduced gene pool, a fact that weakens their resistance to the insects and diseases that plague them.

There is nothing wrong with grafting per se; indeed, large and small growers depend on it to increase their stock. But while heirloom growers use grafts to increase genetic diversity, the large commercial producers are relying on the same shallow pool of apple genes. The 9,000 cultivars of *M. domestica* known today may seem like a large number, but it is a fraction of the number that was once produced worldwide. In the U.S. alone, some 16,000 different varieties were grown in the late nineteenth century. Today, the number is about 3,000. Yet even that number is greatly misleading, since only about a dozen varieties make up 90 per cent of all the apples sold in the country – and nearly half of those are Red Delicious.[38] Thousands of lesser-known varieties, including heirloom seedlings and scions, are available for the asking in nursery catalogues, but the choices in supermarkets remain limited because the apple industry, pressurized by global competition, continues to depend on the best-selling hybrids.

While Red Delicious has been losing its share of the market since its heyday in the 1980s, it remains the single most common variety produced in Washington State, the largest apple-producing state in the USA, and still has a firm foothold in the worldwide market.

Furthermore, most of the new best-sellers, such as Gala and Fuji, are the incestuous offspring of Red Delicious and the other long-reigning members of the apple aristocracy: Golden Delicious, McIntosh and Jonathan. The story is similar in other apple-growing countries. Britain once produced more than 2,500 varieties of apple on thousands of farms. Today it imports 70 per cent of its apples, largely from the same limited roster of mass-produced cultivars. As a result, the number of its own farms has been drastically reduced to a few hundred of significance.[39] Increasing numbers of small orchards in the UK and U.S. are reviving local heirloom apples, but many also produce the best-selling varieties in order to meet public demand. The home-grown Golden Delicious, McIntosh, Gala, Fuji and other big names now offered at farm stands are much fresher than those shipped from distant producers, but the choice still largely consists of the same old standbys.

Like the Irish potato of the nineteenth century and the American elm of the early twentieth century, the monoculture of today's apples has moved forwards in the face of increasing peril – a looming threat of disaster if the cultivars being grown today fall prey to a new, unchecked or uncheckable strain of disease. On the whole, commercial apple breeding has been much more successful in controlling the appearance and storage capability of apples than it has been in creating disease-resistant varieties. Apple growers have used chemical weapons for more than a century to fight the recurrent insect infestations and diseases. During this time, the bugs have kept on evolving, honing their resistance to the latest chemicals. Some of the most popular fungicides used to control apple scab, for example, have lost their ability to ward off this highly destructive disease, which causes ugly lesions on the fruit.[40] Once the lesions crack, they allow insects, other fungi and bacteria into the fruit, thus potentially destroying an entire year's crop. The more potent fungicides require frequent application and are more expensive.

Researchers have learned how to transfer genes from one variety of apple to another, from other kinds of plant and even from insects and animals, to make apples tough enough to fight off scab and other diseases. But the public, rightly or wrongly, remains sceptical if not downright hostile to genetic engineering, especially between different species. Today most growers reluctantly find themselves relying on chemical warfare on a scale never waged before, and at ever-escalating cost. Organic and ecological methods are making only a small dent in the chemical barrage. Old apple trees, the descendants of nearly extinct varieties, are also being lost to the continuing transformation of rural land and forests into roads, housing and commercial buildings in many parts of the world, including swathes of the ancient apple forests of Kazakhstan. To ensure the future of the apple, researchers and orchardists are looking back to its origins, seeking ways to replicate its natural strengths.

Anonymous 17th-century Chinese woodblock print of apples. Today's apples
originated millions of years ago on the mountain ranges of Asia.

three

The Search for Sweetness

Apples pop up in so many cultures over so many periods of history that it is difficult to pinpoint where or when they became part of the human diet. As Henry Thoreau observed, 'It is remarkable how closely the history of the apple-tree is connected with that of man.'[1] Wild crab apples are native to many parts of the temperate world. Their carbonized remains, most likely *Malus sylvestris*, have been discovered in Neolithic and Bronze Age sites throughout Europe.[2] But the sweet domesticated apple, *M. domestica*, has been traced to a specific home. Its evolutionary journey, according to theories based on fossilized plants, began aeons ago when primitive shrubs of the rose family, the first flowering plants on Earth, migrated from North America across the Bering land bridge to central China.[3] As the Eurasian land mass broke apart, submerging the land bridge and forming separate continents, the primal roses and their bitter fruits eventually found new homes. Their seeds were dispersed over wide areas, voided by birds, carried in their beaks or simply stuck to their feet and feathers. The seeds that dropped on to the mountain slopes and foothills of central China could not have found a more hospitable environment for survival and growth. Later known as the Tian Shan Mountains, this area, which now includes Kazakhstan, became a natural refuge for plants and animals. While glaciers spread across western and central Europe, the deadly ice spared the Tian Shan. Its forests and vegetation thrived with ample supplies of water running down from the snowy peaks. Apple trees grew and evolved in the crevasses and along the slopes of the mountains.

Even today, after ski resorts and dachas have overtaken large swathes of the Kazakh forests, the extent and variety of the trees is extraordinary and has astonished visitors, including those familiar with acres of modern commercial orchards. In the late 1990s, Frank Browning left his Kentucky orchard to tour the forests of Kazakhstan. He found 'a variety of wild fruit that the European or American wanderer has never imagined . . . almost like a journey back into an unkempt primordial garden.'[4] Apples are not the only fruit trees growing here, yet other recent visitors described 'entire forests of apples, three-hundred-year-old trees fifty feet tall and as big around as oaks, some of them bearing apples as large and red as modern cultivated varieties'.[5] While many of the trees in the Tian Shan bear sweet apples, each one is different in some small way, in its fruit, flower, growth habit or branches.[6] One can only imagine the vast expanse and immense variation of these apple forests before they were touched by man.

For many years botanists believed that the ancestor of *M. domestica* was *M. sylvestris*, the wild crab apple. Genetic analysis proved otherwise, however. The true ancestor turned out to be *M. sierversii*, the species that still flourishes in the forests of the Tian Shan. Discovered there by a German-Russian botanist, Johann Sievers, in 1793, it has amazing variability in size, taste, shape, colour and texture, the infinite combination of characteristics that reside in the genes of today's sweet-apple seeds. Sievers died before he could trace his discovery to the cultivated apples of the day, and this connection was not revealed until the twentieth century.

How did *M. sieversii* travel from its remote homeland to orchards all over the world? We can first thank the bears and horses of the Tian Shan, which ate the fruit and spread the seeds along their migratory grazing paths. These paths became part of the Silk Road, the fabled route between China and Europe that traders used from about 120 BC until the early Middle Ages. Not just a single route, the Silk

Road was a network of paths followed by caravans of camels and horses across the deserts of western China, through the mountain ranges of today's Kazakhstan and Kyrgyzstan, and over the steppes of Central Asia to the Caspian Sea and beyond. Traders passing through the Tian Shan Mountains on their journeys between East and West most likely picked up the largest apples. Their horses ate the discarded cores and fallen fruit, or pressed them into the soil with their powerful hooves. While camels also travelled along the Silk Road, they had little or no role in distributing apples or any other seeds. Unlike horses and bears, camels masticate and regurgitate food so thoroughly that even the smallest seed has as much chance of passing intact through a camel's gut as the proverbial camel has of passing through the eye of a needle.[7]

To the Chinese, the Silk Road was known as the Horse Road. In the earliest days of travel along this ancient route, China's capital was in the western-central part of the country; as maritime navigation expanded in the fourteenth and fifteenth centuries, China's political centre shifted east to Beijing and the coast. Although part of the Tian Shan range lies within the present borders of China, the adjacent Gobi Desert became a formidable barrier to the spread of apples into the more developed parts of eastern China. The Chinese of the Far East had many fruits, and did not place much value on growing apples.[8] The eastern dynasties had little control over the wild northwestern part of the continent, and the fruit from the Tian Shan migrated more easily to the west.

The apple's history of forage and cultivation by man spans thousands of years and reveals a gradual culinary change from wild to sweet apples. Dried apples were found in the Sumerian tomb of Queen Puabi (*c.* 2600 BC), a testament to their high value. In the Near East in the third and second millennia BC, apples were used in cooking and medicine, and also as love charms.[9] By the time of Cyrus the Great (*c.* 580–529 BC), sweet apples were carefully cultivated in walled gardens throughout the great Persian Empire, which stretched not only through today's Middle East, but also

north to the Caucasus and up into Central Asia, where sweet apples grew wild.

Through war and peace, murder and miscegenation, the sweet apple spread along with the clashing and merging civilizations of Europe. After he conquered Persia in 334 BC, Alexander the Great brought back both sweet apples and skilled Persian gardeners, who taught the Greeks how to grow them. Apples became so common that they were used as missiles in simulated sea battles by the crews aboard Alexander's royal fleet. Those might have been wild rather than cultivated apples, yet, to serve as projectiles, they must have been bigger than little crabs.[10] But the sour crabs remained an important source of food, particularly for the poor. Apples would become a sign of class distinction between those who ate the cultivated ones and those who foraged for the wild varieties. Not long after Alexander's Persian victory, the Greek poet Archestratus wrote *The Life of Luxury* (c. 330 BC), a culinary tale in verse that described the preparation of fine foods in the Mediterranean region. He does not include apples; instead he snobbishly dismisses them as a cheap staple eaten only by the poor.[11] Apparently, he was referring to wild, bitter apples, not the cultivated ones that would eventually become a staple of a well-fed Roman household.

As the Romans perfected the art of grafting in their fruit orchards, vineyards and olive groves, the cultivated apple became a fruit of luxury, eaten as the sweet culmination of bountiful banquets. Often enjoyed outdoors under the branches of extensive apple orchards on great estates, the fruit was also an esteemed feature of interior decoration. In the homes of Pompeii, preserved after the volcanic eruption of AD 79, wall paintings and mosaics prominently display apples. They fill glass bowls overflowing with fruit and are strung in garlands draped over the figure of Cupid.[12] As their empire advanced, the Romans planted apple orchards throughout western Europe and

opposite: Marble statuette of Aphrodite holding an apple. Rome, second century AD. The ancient Romans perfected apple growing and the fruit took root in their mythology.

Britain. They must have found the wild apples growing there distasteful, but the Celts apparently had some sweet apples, either cultivated or chance seedlings, before the Romans arrived. Celtic place names, especially in France, such as Avallon in Burgundy and Aveluy in Picardy, suggest the cultivation of this rare and treasured sweet fruit.[13] After the fall of Rome, the trees in many cultivated sweet-apple orchards crossed with wild seedlings, giving apples a bitter reputation for generations to come.

While in the West many of the old grafted orchards were overtaken by a new wild generation of trees, fruit orchards continued to receive careful attention in the East. In the former Persian Empire, the art of apple cultivation never faltered, even as the followers of Islam took over in the seventh and eighth centuries. Unlike the invaders of the Roman Empire, Muslims valued scholarship, gardening and fruit growing. They tended the old orchards, established new ones in Spain, and also translated and updated the ancient Greek and Roman horticultural texts, adding to their own knowledge and preserving the ancient arts for the future. Charlemagne may have seen and tasted the fruit of Islamic orchards while on crusades in Moorish Spain. By the end of his reign as Holy Roman Emperor (AD 742–814), he ruled the whole of France, much of today's Germany and Austria, and most of Italy. In the year 800, he issued a decree, *Capitulare de villis*, listing the plants and trees to be grown in each town to provide food and herbal medicine. The list included many different types of apple, both sweet and acidic, for eating, drinking and preserving.[14]

Godly Apples

Apple growing became more common in Britain after 1066, once the invading Normans instilled the French enthusiasm for cider into British cuisine. The eleventh century was also a time when Western merchants, pilgrims and scholars began to venture into the Islamic world. Drawn by trade, religious zeal and the advances of Arabic horticulture and medical science, they brought back knowledge and

An English commemorative plate with Adam and Eve and the apple, dated 1635.

goods, not least new varieties of plant, including bulbs and fruit trees. Among the many horticultural introductions, apple trees first found their way back to the West through the gardens of the monasteries and palaces of Europe. Cistercian monks, members of a branch of the Benedictine order that valued manual labour and self-sufficiency, were especially effective in renewing the cultivation of apples across Europe in the twelfth century. They shared grafts from one orchard to another, spreading the apple along with the development of their abbeys in Scotland, Germany, Sweden, Portugal and the eastern Mediterranean.[15]

Apples became an essential element in diet and culture, and, once again, religious developments promoted their popularity as Protestantism spread during the sixteenth century. 'Everywhere that Protestantism took root and climate allowed, orcharding followed', Joan Morgan and Alison Richards maintain in *The Book of Apples* (1993); 'of all the tree fruits it was the apple that appealed to Protestant sensibilities most.'[16] Although the fruit had forced Adam and Eve out of Paradise, Bible-reading Protestants were eager to repair the damage of the Fall through hard work and self-denial. And what better fruit than the apple on which to focus their labour? Easy to grow and cook in many different ways, simple, nourishing and refreshing, not lush like Mediterranean fruit, apples were the staple of rich and poor households alike. Happily, apples grew best in the areas where Protestantism took root, in northern and eastern Europe and in the New World colonies where Protestants fled the backlash of Catholic rule. In 1597, when the British barber-surgeon John Gerard published his first herbal, there were so many apple varieties available that he felt it was impossible for himself or anyone else to distinguish them all:

> I hear of one that intendeth to write a peculiar volume of Apples, and the use of them; yet when he hath done what he can do, he hath done nothing touching their several kinds to distinguish them. This that hath been said shall suffice for our history.[17]

By the seventeenth century, apples had also become a fashion statement. In the elaborate gardens of manor houses and palaces, dwarf varieties were artfully placed in geometric patterns in raised parterres and trained into espaliers and arches. Inside these grand homes, the apple was a decorative feature of carved woodwork and plaster ceilings, just as it had been in the murals and mosaics of Pompeii.[18]

Apples were so important that European and British colonists could not envision living without them, and brought seeds and scions of their favourite varieties to the New World. So it was that millions of years after the primitive ancestors of apple trees migrated from North America to the mountains of Central Asia, the sweet apple returned to the newly discovered continent as a cultivated transplant. Colonists and explorers continued to spread it to other far-flung continents. The Spanish and Portuguese brought it to South America, where it proliferated so vigorously that when Charles Darwin landed in Chile in 1835, he found apple trees growing all along the coast. In 1654 the head of the Dutch East India Company's trading post at

Derbyware porcelain figure of an African woman holding an apple, 1770s. A mark of luxury in the English home, decorative pieces such as this one also offered a touch of the exotic for apple desserts.

Apple wallpaper designed by William Morris, 1877.

Cape Town brought apples to South Africa, and, as Charlemagne had done and as future generations of American landowners would do, made fruit growing a requirement for settlers. It became a major industry there after the British empire builder Cecil Rhodes bought up bankrupt vineyards in the 1890s and converted them to apple orchards.

English sea captains brought apples to Australia in 1788. The trees took root that year, when Captain Arthur Phillip founded the English settlement of Port Jackson, now Sydney, and when the notorious

Captain William Bligh anchored his ship, the *Bounty*, off the coast of Tasmania. The ship's botanist planted three apple seedlings and apple and pear seeds on the island, which later became known as 'Apple Isle'.[19] These early efforts were literally the seeds of the booming apple industry in Australia and New Zealand, countries that now enjoy a reverse-season advantage in supplying fruit to Americans, Europeans and Canadians during the northern hemisphere's winter.

A tasty apple in winter is greatly appreciated today, but it was even more important in the days when fresh fruit was only a seasonal treat. 'People of my grandparents' and great grandparents' generation', the apple orchardist Ezekiel Goodband recalls, 'did not have the luxury of fresh fruit year-round; the only apples available at that time of year would be dried or the last apples in the bottom of a barrel in the root cellar.'[20] The arrival of the first apples of the season ended the long winter months with a sweet, fresh taste of summer. Wealthy Victorian landowners with greenhouses and large gardening staffs enjoyed apples all year round.

The nineteenth century was an explosive time for apple production in Britain, Europe and America, and new types were hailed with the kind of passionate reviews now directed at films and popular music.[21] The number of new varieties increased along with agricultural improvements, inspiring horticulturalists to catalogue the bounty. The three-volume *Pomological Magazine* (1828–30), produced by the British botanist John Lindley with hand-coloured engravings and detailed descriptions, was one of many beautifully illustrated inventories of apples and other fruit that appeared during this age of great enthusiasm for gardening and botanical painting.

In the second half of the century, as English apple growers struggled to stem the rising tide of imported apples reaching its shores, the Scottish nurseryman Robert Hogg created several manuals for growers covering all the fruits grown in Britain, from apples to walnuts. In his last, of 1884, he documented more than 700 varieties of apple in a highly detailed account that remains the standard reference for old English varieties.[22] In 1905 the U.S. Government Printing Office

Poster for New Zealand apples, *c.* 1920s–30s.

published *Nomenclature of the Apple*, a compilation of the names of about 16,000 varieties listed in nineteenth-century American publications.

But in the second half of the twentieth century, the competitive economics of agribusiness whittled down the number of well-known varieties to a relative handful. Most of the names in the antique rosters of apples are no longer familiar. Even the varieties that many adults today grew up with and that were once synonymous with apples, such as the Baldwin – once the most popular apple in New England and New York, and one of their biggest exports – have been absent for more than half a century from grocers and super-markets, replaced by the best-selling and insipidly sweet Red Delicious. England remains one of the few countries where a tart cooking apple, the historic Bramley's Seedling, is still a major variety of the commercial market. In some regions of Europe, such as the cider-producing areas of northern France and Spain, speciality vari-eties are also still in demand. But these are exceptions in the global market of uniform apples.

'A Hoary Morning Apple', from the 19th-century *British Fruit at Anglesey Abbey* by John Lindley, one of the many beautifully illustrated inventories of apples and other fruits that appeared during this age of great enthusiasm for gardening and botanical painting.

Selling apples on Main Street on Saturday afternoon, Lexington, Mississippi, 1939.

Leon Augustin L'Hermitte, *The Market Place of Ploudalmezeau*, c. 1877, oil on canvas, a scene of villagers in Brittany selling apples and vegetables.

Papier mâché figurine of a skeleton seller of toffee apples used in the Mexican Day of the Dead Festival, c. 1980s. Many apples today are bred very sweet to compete with sugary treats.

For years toffee apples, also called candy apples or caramel apples, have been a popular treat. They are ubiquitous at Halloween in the U.S. and are even sold by vendors on the beaches of Mexico and Palestine. The sweet coverings often hide the taste of a mealy apple, but even without sugar coatings, some commercial apples, such as those in the supersweet category, are being bred to compete with sweets and candy themselves. The sweet apple has come a long way from the mountains of the Tian Shan only to end up, as the food writer Michael Pollan has said, in a 'sweetness arms race with junk food'.[23] Yet the race has slowed somewhat with the growth of heirloom apples, as mass-produced fruit continues to stir a new hunger for the lost flavours of the past.

Silver escutcheon with pierced lettering for bottled cider, *c.* 1750, London. The fancy design reflects the high regard for bottled cider at this time.

Snow-covered crab apples. Henry Thoreau believed that frozen apples made the best cider.

four

Cider Chronicles

❧

Wherever people ate apples, they also drank cider. It is one of the oldest alcoholic drinks known to man. Unlike the production of beer and whisky, a process that requires the harvesting of wheat or hops, as well as hulling, grinding and heating before fermentation, apples turn into cider virtually on their own. If the fruit is left to rot, its natural sugar and yeast yield a ready-made alcoholic drink. Bears that eat quantities of the rotten fruit have been observed with a tipsy gait. Henry Thoreau also enjoyed apple cider naturally processed in the wild:

> Let the frost come to freeze them first, solid as stones, and then the rain or a warm winter day to thaw them, and they will seem to have borrowed a flavor from heaven through the medium of the air in which they hang . . . better than any bottled cider that I know of . . . All apples are good in this state, and your jaws are the cider-press.[1]

In Thoreau's time, cider in America was primarily an alcoholic drink, as it still is everywhere else in the world where it is consumed. Today, Americans call the alcoholic version 'hard cider' to distinguish it from the unfermented beverage, known simply as cider or sweet cider, which is much more widely available in the U.S. The change was part of cider's roller-coaster history. From ancient times to the present, the alcoholic version has been extolled, reviled and, most recently, revived. The Greeks and Romans developed crushing and pressing equipment to make it, and, unlike many of their horticultural developments, these techniques were not buried by the Dark Ages. Cider eventually became a national beverage, a method of payment and barter, and an alternative to wine in both Europe and America.

Although it was the conquering Normans who popularized *cidre* in Britain, cider became a British beverage of 'patriotic self-sufficiency' during the Hundred Years War (1337–1453), when France blocked shipments of wine.[2] During the Protestant Reformation of the sixteenth century, Puritans praised cider because they saw the apple as morally preferable to the grape, the source of wine used in what they considered the 'corrupt' Catholic Mass. Oliver Cromwell's Puritan government strongly supported the planting of fruit orchards, and one of his agents, Samuel Hartlib, along with other agricultural reformers, believed that 'every spare piece of ground should be filled with apples'.[3] In his treatise *A Design for Plentie, By an Universal Planting of Fruit-trees* (1652), Hartlib maintained that apples would provide 'for the relief of the poor, the benefit of the rich, and the delight of all'.[4] Fifty years earlier, John Gerard had said much the same thing in his *Herball*. He advised all English landholding gentlemen to follow the example of a Hereford man whose servants 'drink no other drink but that which is made of apples', and who paid his tithe to the parson in 'many hogsheads of Syder':[5]

> Graffe [graft], set, plant and nourish up trees in every corner of your ground; the labour is small, the cost is nothing, the commodity is great, your selves shall have plenty, the poore shall have somewhat in time of want to relieve their necessity, and God shall reward your good mindes and diligence.[6]

The English gentry must have taken this advice to heart, particularly in Herefordshire and other parts of the West Country where apple

opposite: Crushing apples for cider, Normandy, 1928.

Cider glasses, *c.* 1760–70, Bristol. While the working class drank their cider from crude pottery mugs, the wealthy drank it, like champagne, from decorative stemware.

growing flourished. By the end of the seventeenth century, cider was the beverage of choice for men of wealth and taste. But their guiding principle was not God's rewards, but a belief in superior English methods. Cider's greatest proponent of the day, John Worlidge, a horticulturalist influenced by the scientific methods of the Enlightenment, catalogued British apples in a comprehensive treatise of 1676 and evaluated them for the finest cider, as the French had done with grapes for fine wines. Worlidge and other specialists, including members of the Royal Society, sought to prove that British ciders would eventually surpass continental wines. Cider was generally fermented in wooden barrels and drawn off in draughts, but sturdy glass bottles developed around this time produced naturally sparkling cider, almost like apple Champagne, that could be shipped and poured at stylish parties in London.[7]

During the course of the next two centuries, economic and agricultural changes would once again change cider and the standards of taste. Worlidge's high hopes for British cider were undone by the inevitable forces of commerce. Many producers diluted the first pressing, or put the pomace through a second time with water to moisten it, something that poor farmers had always done to stretch limited harvests. The weak result was known as ciderkin, or water cider, but water was not the only addition. Other fruits, fresh or spoiled, and even animal parts might be added to ferment the mix into a rough brew known as 'scrumpy'. The English botanist Thomas Andrew Knight, another Herefordshire man known for his love of apples, tried to improve the quality of cider in the late eighteenth century.

While the well-to-do enjoyed the finer vintages, the flood of cheap cider continued to dilute the economic value of the market, and by the 1870s apple growing was not nearly as profitable as the farming of other crops. Many farmers uprooted their orchards or simply ignored them, leaving the untended trees for labourers and the poor to harvest. Paying wages for farm labour in cider had been common practice in the eighteenth century – two quarts a day for a man and one quart for a boy – until it was made illegal in 1878.[8] Before long, gin, beer and factory-produced cider began to flow more freely in public houses, and fashionable English society turned once again to wine.

Sinful Cider

Cider in America also has an up-and-down history, but it was a surge of moral outrage that washed the alcohol out of the traditional drink. Raised on alcoholic cider in Europe, American settlers started producing their own soon after they arrived in the New World. According to the American apple historian and nurseryman Tom Burford, 'by the 1650s, apple orchards with thousands of trees had been planted – specifically for cider.'[9] By 1820, every farmer with a few apple trees was producing cider for his own use or trading it for goods; larger producers were selling it to taverns, and everyone was drinking it. But over the next decades, many orchards were abandoned as the

New apple cider sign. Ever since the Temperance Movement raged through the U.S. in the 19th century, American apple cider, like that advertised at this farm stand in Cambridge, New York, has been unfermented.

Industrial Revolution drew farmers to the city. And when they went to the local saloons, they did not find cider. The flow of German and Irish immigrants to the U.S. in the mid-nineteenth century, along with cheap grain from the American Midwest, made beer and whiskey the working man's drinks. Apple cider was made on small farms and did not travel well; meanwhile German immigrants were setting up large breweries in the cities, producing vast quantities of beer, the drink often provided as refreshment for labourers in hot, crowded factories.

Contending with wretched housing and working conditions in the cities, many labourers and their families fell into a vicious cycle of poverty, alcoholism and domestic abuse. In the face of these growing problems, the Temperance Movement, made up of thousands of groups trying to curb or outlaw alcohol, soared to new heights of activity in the U.S. While beer and whiskey were most often the culprits, the outcry against alcohol eventually targeted cider as well. Initially, the movement sought a ban on the production of the more potent liquors, but the cause was deeply embedded in nineteenth-century American morality and it eventually stained the reputation of American apple growers. Arguments against cider were framed in religious terms. Those against it accused farmers who sold their apples for cider of serving Mammon rather than God. Farmers who had been producing cider for their own family's use for generations argued that it was a sin to waste God's bounty. But the moralists maintained that the only righteous path for a Christian farmer raising apple trees was to burn them.[10]

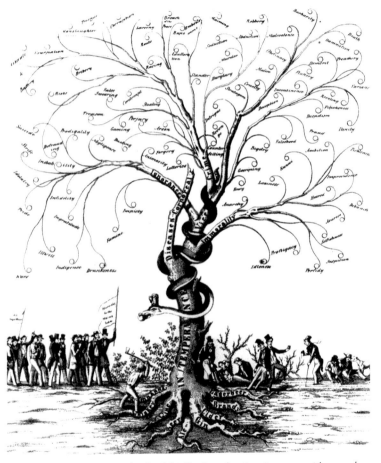

'Benefits of temperance and evils of drink', 1850s drawing. A serpent with an apple in its mouth and a mug of beer on its head winds around the trunk. The branches represent a plethora of social and moral evils: wars, drunkenness, anarchy and so on. On the left, a procession of men march with banners supporting Prohibition, and on the right, a group of men are collapsing in states of inebriation.

The best-known figure of the American Temperance Movement is the hatchet-wielding teetotaller Carrie Nation, a formidable woman of imposing size and fearless determination. Standing nearly 1.8 m (6 ft) tall and weighing close to 90 kg (200 lb), she led her female followers into saloons in the first decade of the twentieth century, crying 'Smash, ladies, smash!' as they attacked the bars and furniture with their hatchets. The movement drew members from every rung of society, including the wealthiest. One of the biggest supporters was the richest man in America, John D. Rockefeller, the founder of the powerful Standard Oil monopoly. Anti-alcoholic consumption was a core belief of many Baptists, including the Rockefellers, who pursued the cause with evangelical fervour. Rockefeller's wife, Celestia, was a founder in 1878 of what became the most influential temperance group, the Women's Christian Temperance Union, the largest women's organization in the country. Despite the privileged status of her wealth, Celestia would enter saloons and get down on her knees to pray for 'sodden sinners'.[11]

The image of hatchet-wielding teetotallers destroying not just saloons but also apple trees became part of New England folklore in the nineteenth and early twentieth centuries. It is easy to picture scores of trees being chopped down in Thoreau's reaction to the loss of orchards in New England: 'I now, alas, speak rather from memory than from any recent experience, such ravages have been made!'[12] But many churchgoing farmers, weary of being castigated for their evil ways, had simply abandoned their orchards.[13] The toll was not only in cider. Many of the old apple varieties were lost, and without their tart–sweet complexity, the trend was set for milder-flavoured apples and overly sweet, unfermented cider.

The song 'Sipping Cider Through a Straw' was published in 1919, the year the National Prohibition Act banning the manufacture, transportation and sale of 'intoxicating liquors' was introduced in the U.S. Congress. The lyrics painted a very different picture from the evil days of drinking alcoholic cider:

The prettiest girl I ever saw
      Was sippin' cider through a straw. . . .
Then cheek to cheek
And jaw to jaw
We sipped that cider
Through a straw.
And now and then
That straw would slip
And I'd sip some cider
From her lip
And now I've got
A mother-in-law
From sipping cider
Through a straw.

The song was either a bit of nostalgia for the old days or an effort to create an innocent image for cider. Either way, by 1919 the days of farmers growing apples solely for cider in the USA were long gone. Fifteen years earlier, J. T. Stinson, a fruit specialist at the World's Fair of 1904 in St Louis, Missouri, had proclaimed 'an apple a day keeps the doctor away', a marketing device to erase cider's negative history and promote the market for fresh apples. Even the Nazi government promoted apples as a health food, and began Germany's first large-scale production of apple juice.[14]

American Prohibition, enacted in 1920, did allow a certain amount of 'non-intoxicating cider' to be made in the home. Of course, left for a few days it would begin to ferment on its own. A cartoon of the day depicts a farmer making cider in his orchard while men dressed in city clothes lean over the fence and ask if he needs any help. During this notorious period of U.S. history, the Federal Bureau of Investigation famously hunted down criminals who made their fortunes and reputations with illegal liquor. No one ever accused Al Capone or any of the other big-time bootleggers of selling 'intoxicating' cider, but, nonetheless, the FBI also burned down some cider apple orchards during Prohibition.[15]

Prohibition cartoon. Published in 1919, the year Prohibition began in the U.S., this is a caricature of the law's allowance of alcoholic cider made at home for personal use.

To Your Health

The FBI and teetotallers would never admit it, but fermented cider was actually good for you. It may have been an alcoholic enticement, but it also had a long history as a healthy, lifesaving drink. John Worlidge believed that 'not any drink was more effectual against Scurvy, against the stone [kidney stones], disease of spleen . . . and excellent against Melancholy.'[16] Drinking alcoholic cider no doubt lifted one's spirits, but it also had other demonstrable benefits. Fermentation retained enough vitamin C to prevent scurvy incurred on long sea voyages. It also produced vitamin B12, a lifesaver for medieval European peasants and for rural farmers in colonial America during the long winters without meat or fresh fruit and vegetables. In the nineteenth century, American farmers would add corn whiskey to partially fermented cider to bring up the alcohol content and kill off bacteria. This made it a safer drink than the questionably drinkable water from wells, which at times were polluted by animal and human waste.

Ironically, the alcoholic version of cider also proved to be a safer drink than some of the unfermented cider sold in modern times. In 1996 a sixteen-month-old girl died after drinking a beverage made from sweet apple cider that had been contaminated with the E. coli bacterium; scores of others in the U.S. were made ill by the same brand. The bacteria were traced to fallen apples that had been contaminated by faecal matter from animals grazing in the orchards. The shocking events led to strict government regulations, including the requirement for pasteurization, a process that kills off both the bacteria and the vitamins, and requires expensive equipment. (Vitamin C, lost through exposure to heat, oxygen and light, is often reintroduced into the cider after processing.) Ultraviolet treatment, a more affordable alternative for small producers, was later determined to be as effective as pasteurization in destroying pathogens.

Cider makers today maintain that the only way to ensure safe cider is to require higher-quality fruit and more thorough hygiene. 'If you start with bad fruit and unclean processing, it's hard to understand

Pasteurized sweet cider. After a child died from drinking sweet cider in 1996, most of that produced in the U.S. has been pasteurized, a process that kills both bacteria and vitamin C.

how heat-treating the juice is supposed to make it any more drinkable', David Buchanan, an heirloom cider maker in Maine, explains.[17] Although pasteurizing cider is not a government regulation in the UK, the process is used by some large commercial producers to stabilize fermentation, stopping it so that the cider doesn't turn into vinegar. Many artisanal cider makers are highly critical of the process, along with other procedures considered to be artificial. In 1988, the UK organization CAMRA (Campaign for Real Ale) expanded its efforts to promoting 'real cider'. The target of its disdain is the prevalence of keg cider, which is generally pasteurized, artificially carbonated, supplemented with additives and colourings, and often made with apple concentrate rather than 'real apples'.[18] Apple concentrates, used in both apple cider and juice, have brought about additional concerns in the UK and the U.S. Chinese apple concentrates dominate the world market, and in 2013 three of China's leading producers were found to be using rotten apples, which carry the risk of toxic moulds.[19] Cider makers in Germany and France have a long history of producing

Théophile Emmanuel Duverger, *New Cider*, mid-19th century, drawing.
Cider fresh from the press is being offered to the baby.

the drink with locally grown apples and without pasteurization or artificial additives. German cider, known as *Apfelwein*, is generally a sour, tart drink compared to the relatively sweet British and American cider. Although French cider makers face an uphill battle against wine, several producers in Normandy are still making cider today with all the care of fine winemakers.[20]

Making a Comeback

Prohibition in the USA ended in 1933, but it was too late for fermented cider to make a comeback with Americans, whose thirst for alcohol had been slaked by beer and other booze. Yet in the last decade of the century, tastes began to change once again. Like the renewed interest in growing heirloom apples, the production of alcoholic cider has experienced astonishing growth since it was reintroduced to the U.S. market in the 1990s. Sales in 2007 alone were 200 per cent higher than in the previous year.[21] This is good news for heirloom

Barrel-brewed cider. Many artisanal ciders made today are brewed the old-fashioned way in oak barrels.

growers, who can sell their apples to cider makers for more money than they earn selling them at farm stalls and to fancy food shops. In this age of gluten-free diets, cider also has an advantage over wheat-based drinks.

'Cider is at once the humblest of uses for the apple . . . and its most forgiving', Buchanan maintains.[22] Compared to wine, it is relatively easy for domestic gardeners to make their own cider, as generations of small farmers did, and it is a growing pastime for foodies with homes in the country. But cider making is predominantly on the rise among artisanal producers who, like many craft-beer brewers and young chefs, are dedicated to reviving fresh, flavourful food, sourced to the greatest degree possible from locally grown crops. Like keg cider in the UK, bottled alcoholic cider – pasteurized, made with preservatives and sweetened with corn syrup – has been available in the U.S. for some time, but the popularity of the 'all natural', drier versions is relatively new.

One of the most interesting U.S. brand names, considering America's cider history, is Original Sin. Developed in 1997 in upstate New York, it was one of the first handcrafted ciders to break into the beer market in Manhattan. The young man who created it, Gideon Coll, started out by lugging cases of his cider on New York City subways and handing out single bottles to bar owners to convince them to stock it. The brand is now sold throughout the country and in the UK and Japan. The company also produces Newtown Pippin cider, a 'single heirloom varietal' made exclusively from New York City's famous apple of the eighteenth century.[23] In 2011 New York State counted some 200 hard cider producers, the highest number in the nation. But Coll's story is typical of artisanal cider makers in several other apple-growing states who began by selling to a market unfamiliar with the drink.

Britain leads the world in cider drinking, in large part because of Percy Bulmer, who began making factory-produced alcoholic cider in 1888 in a warehouse in Hereford.[24] Bulmers is now the world's leading cider maker, but handcrafted brands are enjoying booming sales in English and Irish pubs, and are also on the rise in other countries.[25] As recently as 2006, the idea of visiting cider mills seemed curious compared to that of visiting wineries. The author of an article in *Gourmet* magazine that year, about artisanal mills in Quebec, had to convince readers that the trip to these rural outposts was worthwhile. The mills included unique operations, including one that produced ice cider by allowing apples to freeze on the tree and then pressing them still frozen, a method similar to the one described more than a century ago by Thoreau. Knowing that readers would be sceptical, the writer began the article by asking, 'Is cider really complex and

A tractor sweeps up apples in a Herefordshire orchard, 2009,
a historic cider-making county in the west of England.

compelling enough to lure you . . . to a dozen or so *cidreries*?'[26] The
growing number of cider drinkers today would no doubt say 'yes'.
Quebec has continued the age-old French tradition of making *cidre*
established in Canada by French settlers in the sixteenth century.
Spain's bubbly, dry *sidra*, traditionally poured from a height to create
a frothy drink, also never went out of style, particularly in the Basque
region. Cider is even becoming popular in Mexico, where it was
traditionally drunk only at Christmas.[27]

Beer producers in the U.S. and UK are taking advantage of the
growing market by buying up or starting their own cider brands.
Gregory Hall, the former brewmaster for Chicago's Goose Island
Beer, left the company in 2011 to start Virtue Cider in Michigan and
is now producing several craft ciders based on European methods.
Some of the biggest beer companies in the industry have also got in
on the act: Molson Coors bought Crispin cider and launched Redd's
Apple Ale; Boston Beer now produces Angry Orchard; the C&C
Group, the Irish producer of Magners cider, bought Vermont's
Woodchuck Cider; and most recently Stella Artois, owned by the giant
Anheuser-Busch, maker of Budweiser, launched Stella Artois *Cidre*.[28]

It has been available in England for a few years, but 'the decision to bring it across the Atlantic counts as a ringing endorsement for the future of cider-drinking in the States', according to Andrew Knowlton, restaurant and drinks editor for *Bon Appetit* magazine.[29] With its dry, 'European-style' taste and French name, Stella Artois *Cidre* is designed to be an alternative to white wine. The company is also trying to break into a challenging American market by advertising during televised sporting events. Along with guzzling beer and eating burgers and barbecue, drinking '*cidre* from hand-picked apples' is now being promoted to macho football and basketball fans.

A bottling machine for cider, Switzerland, 1934.

U.S. postage stamps commemorating American apples, January 2013.

five

The American Apple

The question that immediately comes to mind about American apples is whether they are truly American. The only apple trees in America when the Europeans arrived were wild crab apples with small, bitter fruit. Considering that the early settlers brought the first apple seedlings and scions of *Malus domestica* from Europe, how did the Yankees later claim the sweet apple as their 'national fruit'? And what about the validity of the widely accepted metaphor, 'as American as apple pie', which ignores the fact that apples baked in pastry had been eaten in Britain and Europe for centuries? Jane Austen, who wrote in a letter to her sister in 1815 'Good apple pies are a considerable part of our domestic happiness', was just one of countless people who did not consider apple pies an exclusively American dish.[1]

All that may be old hat, but America has lots of competition today for national rights to the apple. Surprisingly, even shockingly to most Americans, more than half the world's apples are now grown in China, a looming challenge to the U.S. apple industry. Except for Chinese apple juice, which has flooded the American market as frozen concentrate – more than half of American-produced apple juice is made with Chinese concentrate – the USA has so far kept the tsunami of low-cost, fresh Chinese apples at bay. No longer number one, the USA is the world's second-largest apple producer, but its crop is far behind that of China (it raised 4.2 million tons in 2010; China raised 33.2 million tons in the same year). At some U.S. farm stalls, the plastic

'As American as apple pie', the widely accepted saying, belies the fact that apple pie was standard fare in Britain and Europe centuries before it became an American dish.

bags adorned with red apples and filled with homegrown fruit are made in China, perhaps a sign of things to come. If and when the flood of Chinese apples reaches U.S. shores, would New York City still be the Big Apple? Patriotic pride may have a lot to do with America's continuing claim to the apple, yet there is a long history behind it. Like wine in France, beer in Germany and olive oil in Italy, the apple has long been a significant part of the U.S. economy and culture.

Botanically speaking, there is something to say for sweet apples as American natives, or at least distant cousins to the European varieties. With today's scientific hindsight, it might be said that the transplants were a return of America's native apples, the ancestors of *M. domestica* that began aeons ago when primitive shrubs of the rose family migrated from North America to central China and spread from the nourishing slopes of the Tian Shan Mountains to Europe. But after centuries of grafting in Europe, the trees brought by Old World settlers did not adapt well to different conditions in the New World. The transplants did not last long in the harsh New England winters; however, they did set seeds that grew into trees quite different from their European forebears, trees that were eventually embraced as American natives. Their fruit flourished with help from another European transplant, the honeybee.

North America already had wild bees and other insects that pollinated its wild crab-apple trees, wild flowers and other plants.

An ever-present bowl of apples sits on a table in the Oval Office while U.S. President Barack Obama makes a phone call in the background, 2009. Apples are part of First Lady Michelle Obama's campaign to promote healthy food.

But the early settlers were more familiar with cultivated honeybees, raised for honey and beeswax in man-made hives ever since the days of ancient Egypt. And they must have known, or soon learned from experience, that it was difficult, if not impossible, to gather honey and beeswax from wild bees or to move them into orchards to pollinate their transplanted fruit trees. The Virginia Company, chartered by James I of England in 1606, regularly shipped cows, sheep, chickens and other necessities to its colonies. An invoice dated 1621 from the company to the colony in Jamestown, Virginia, also notes a shipment of what could have been America's first honeybees.[2] Safely contained in hives, they sailed over the Atlantic for six weeks to their new home. Colonists from the Netherlands, Sweden and France also brought honeybees, along with their knowledge of bee-keeping, to North America.

The honeybees formed their own colonies and, like the settlers, swarmed westward, serving as advance troops for the pioneers. Native Americans called the bees 'the white man's flies' and knew that when they began to buzz about, the settlers were not far behind. By the time Johnny Appleseed and other New England migrants reached the frontier of today's Midwest at the end of the eighteenth century, honeybees, well established in hollow trees, were ready to pollinate the newly planted apple seedlings. The bees migrated to the far west at a slower pace. It would take another half century before honeybees reached Utah, carried along with apple seeds and scions by Mormons on covered wagons in 1848. Honeybees finally made it to the west coast in 1853, transported to California over land and sea via Panama by the botanist Christopher A. Shelton.[3] By the 1870s, more than two million apple trees were growing in California.[4]

During the first centuries of America's settlement, apple trees were largely grown from seed, a much cheaper and less labour-intensive method than grafts for small farmers. A few commercial nurseries of the colonial period propagated fruit trees by grafting, in Virginia and at the Prince Nursery of New York, where the Newtown Pippin first appeared as a seedling. Grafts and seedlings were mixed in the orchards to provide different varieties of summer and winter apples. By the eighteenth century, American nurseries were shipping apples to the West Indies and across the Atlantic. Some of America's first apple trees reached Britain through a plant exchange between an American farmer and an English merchant. Beginning in 1733 and continuing for four decades, the Philadelphia farmer John Bartram shipped hundreds of boxes of American seeds, scions and plants to the London plant collector John Collinson, a wealthy merchant who conducted a widespread trade with other horticultural enthusiasts. As Andrea Wulf reveals in *The Brother Gardeners* (2008), 'the American evergreens, magnificent trees and colorful shrubs . . . laid the foundations of the English garden.'[5] The Bartram–Collinson exchange also introduced the Newtown Pippin to London, via Benjamin Franklin, who received a shipment of the variety in 1758 while in London and gave one to his friend Collinson. Impressed by the flavour, Collinson asked Bartram to send him scions of the variety. Its popularity survived him, for in 1768, the year of his death, Brompton Park Nursery in London, England's foremost nursery of the day, was selling the 'Newtown Pippin of New York'. In 1773 Collinson's son reported that while the English apple crop had been disappointing that year, 'American apples had been found an admirable substitute.'[6]

Frontier Apples

In America, more than in any other country, the apple played a major role in national expansion. It was as important to the settlement of the American Midwest as gold was to the settlement of California. Apples did not tempt settlers to travel west, as gold did, but they were the means by which the pioneers literally put down roots. While the pursuit of gold was a flash in the pan of California's demographic development, the apple trees planted on the American frontier of the early eighteenth century (today's Midwestern states of Ohio, Western Pennsylvania, Indiana, Illinois and Michigan) rooted people to the soil. As an early twentieth-century poem about Johnny

The apple played a major role in American expansion.

Appleseed rhapsodized, 'hearts took root in the alien loam, and every orchard became a home.'[7] Tens of thousands of fortune-seekers flocked to California in the Gold Rush of 1849, but only about 10 per cent chose to live in the state.[8] At the same time, settlers and landholding companies were planting apple orchards to stake more lasting claims to the Midwestern territories. But apple growers also struck it rich during the Gold Rush. During its peak of activity, California prospectors hungry for fresh fruit paid five dollars an apple.[9]

John Chapman, the man who became the famous Johnny Appleseed, is credited with leading the apple's conquest of the American frontier. Like so many stories of national origin, America's westward expansion has been romanticized into a nostalgic tale of legendary heroes. Celebrated and oversimplified in children's books and films, Johnny Appleseed and the American apple are part of a much larger story. Unlike the 'ordinary, uncontroversial fruit' of today, the historian William Kerrigan explains, the American apple

> was a fruit suffused with cultural meaning, and at times it served as a symbol in contests between Native Americans and European invaders, between poor whites and richer ones, between the tippler and the teetotaler, and between those embracing the modern age and those nostalgic for the past.[10]

A legend in his own time, Appleseed was also celebrated after his death by a host of American poets, playwrights and novelists. He became even more widely known through a biopic of 1948 by Disney, in which he wears a flour-sack coat and a tin pot on his head while holding a bag of apple seeds. The cartoon is still the best-known image of the man. In both folklore and film, he was portrayed as an altruistic eccentric who ushered apple trees into the wilderness while living a life of saintly self-denial – a sort of St Francis of the Apples.

American writers of the nineteenth and early twentieth centuries, including Carl Sandburg, Edgar Lee Masters and Stephen Vincent Benét, lauded Appleseed, but none was more taken with his mythic qualities than Vachel Lindsay, who saw Appleseed as the 'soul of America and its salvation'.[11] Lindsay wrote numerous mystical poems, songs and stories about him that rose to the point of apotheosis. In his strange novel *The Golden Book of Springfield* (1920), some of Johnny's apple seeds grew into orchards of the 'Apple Amaranth', a fruit that imparted in all who ate it a love of eternal beauty. The book also envisioned Appleseed as a canonized saint in 2018. Even the Disney cartoon had a religious subtext, depicting an angel handing Johnny the bag of apple seeds and sending him on a divinely inspired mission to plant them throughout America.

Chapman was, in fact, a missionary for the Swedenborgian Movement, but since he was the son of a landless father, the incentive for his itinerant livelihood on the frontier was apparently necessity

Johnny Appleseed stamps, 1966, commemorating the legendary figure who planted apple seeds on the U.S. frontier in the mid-19th century.

rather than altruism. He did not get rich selling apple seedlings to settlers, but in the process he acquired a great deal of land on which he established his apple nurseries – some 490 ha (1,200 acres) at one point in his life – and was never poor.[12] Nonetheless, by selling seedlings (called common or natural trees) rather than more expensive grafts, he was seen as a champion of the common man and a symbol of American democracy. Costing just a few pennies each compared to 25 cents for a grafted tree, seedlings were affordable to the poor, and if the stories are correct, the kindly Appleseed gave many away.[13] But his business success did not stop him from wearing shabby clothes and living in primitive shelters in the wilderness. His admirers compared his simple lifestyle to that of a saint, but – since most apples at the time were fermented as cider – Michael Pollan calls Appleseed the 'American Dionysus', the man who 'brought the gift of alcohol to the frontier'.[14]

Appleseed's fame has spread from coast to coast, and his name and image are featured in harvest festivals throughout the country. Since the 1880s, the town of Paradise in northern California has held an annual series of events called 'Johnny Appleseed Days', but the celebrated pioneer never travelled further than the Midwest. In a wider historic context, Kerrigan maintains, the legend of Johnny Appleseed is 'essentially a celebration of American empire – the transformation of a continent from savage to civilized . . . one that ignored the reality of Native American dispossession'.[15] The Appleseed myth portrays him as the only one planting seeds in the wilderness, yet Native Americans and white settlers had cultivated orchards well before him, as S. A. Beach notes:

When once the apple was introduced its dissemination kept pace with the progress of the settlement of the country. In fact, it was carried by Indians, traders and white missionaries far in the wilderness beyond the outermost white settlements. Reports of General Sullivan's expedition, in 1779, against the Cayugas and Senecas, in describing the Indian villages which were then destroyed, make frequent mention of peach and apple orchards that were found bending with fruit.[16]

Sullivan's expedition, a devastating counter-attack against Native American tribes allied with the British during the Revolutionary War, was a scorched-earth campaign that destroyed at least 40 villages in Western New York State. Without their orchards and crops, many of the survivors starved the following winter. In the expansionist years to come, Native American lands that were not brutally overtaken by white forces were reluctantly surrendered in treaties. An heirloom apple recently rediscovered in North Carolina, the Junaluska, is named for a Cherokee Chief who did not want to sell his land to the government because his favourite apple tree grew there. The government eventually gave him an extra $50 for the tree.[17]

Although the Native Americans cleared some land for growing food, they held on to the surrounding forests for hunting grounds.

American apple advertisement, 1920. An ironic and quite unintended reminder that apple orchards planted by white settlers displaced Native Americans in the 19th century.

Once the indigenous people were gone, however, landholding companies bought large tracts of land and leased or donated them to settlers, requiring the pioneers to clear established forests and plant new orchards so that the companies could hold on to their wilderness claims.[18] Many of the mythic stories about Johnny Appleseed portray him as a friend to the Native Americans. Unlike many other Americans moving on to the frontier, he never used violent means against them, but as Kerrigan points out,

> consciously or not, his efforts in planting orchards in the wilderness, along with so many others who helped to settle the frontier, did so by transforming tribal lands and dispossessing the people who depended upon them.[19]

Appleseed loved the wilderness and hated towns, but it is 'uncanny how many of his nursery sites became towns'.[20]

Apples on the Brain

Apples were everywhere in the nineteenth-century New England landscape – and in the zeitgeist. They blossomed in the philosophical, religious and intellectual ideas of the age as symbols used repeatedly by the pre-eminent thinkers, writers and speakers of the region. The most famous were at the forefront of Transcendentalism, a loosely organized set of beliefs focused on the spiritual link between man and the natural world. Henry Thoreau was not the only Transcendentalist who saw the apple as a symbol of the American spirit. Ralph Waldo Emerson and Henry Ward Beecher heaped praise upon the apple, raising its profile to patriotic pride. Emerson, Thoreau's mentor, called it 'our national fruit', and Beecher, a popular preacher, writer and lecturer, said it was, 'beyond all question, the American fruit'.[21] In his lecture 'Political Economy of the Apple', delivered in 1864 to the booming apple-growing state of New York, he could not say enough good things about the fruit:

> It is conceded in Europe that, for size, soundness, flavor, and brilliancy of coloring, the American apple stands first, a long way first . . . But it is American in another sense . . . Of fruits . . . this above all others, may be called the true democratic fruit.[22]

Ironically, many of Beecher's claims for the American apple are similar to those that made the fruit appeal to Protestant sensibilities in Britain and Europe. Like Thoreau and many other Transcendentalists, Beecher was a Protestant whose ethics had been shaped by American patriotism.

> It is so easy of propagation . . . It is neither dainty nor dyspeptic . . . It is naturally tough as an Indian, patient as an ox, and faithful as the Jewish Rachel . . . In short, it is a genuine democrat . . . whether neglected, abused, or abandoned, it is able to take care of itself, and to be fruitful of excellences. That is what I call being democratic. The apple tree is the common people's tree, moreover, because it is the child of every latitude and every longitude on this continent.[23]

Not by Apples Alone

Perhaps no one in this group of American Transcendentalists was more intimately involved with apples than Bronson Alcott (1799–1888), the father of Louisa May Alcott (1832–1888), the author of *Little Women*. Less well-known today than his compatriots Thoreau, Emerson and Beecher, Alcott, an educational reformer, was part of their circle but led a unique apple adventure that nearly took his life. In 1843, after losing his teaching position in Boston because of his liberal views, he and an Englishman of similar mind, Charles Lane, began a small utopian community, which they named Fruitlands. Located in a rural area west of Boston, it was comprised of sixteen members, including Alcott's wife and four daughters, who all lived in a rustic farmhouse surrounded by extensive fields and a scattering of apple and other fruit trees.

Old apple tree at Fruitlands, Harvard, Massachusetts, 2013, a failed utopian community where apples were the main source of food.

Alcott and Lane chose the location as a spiritual retreat from the material world, and planned to live a stoic existence there without any animal products or labour, which they believed amounted to stealing from poor beasts. Apples and bread were among the few foods they considered pure enough to comply with their ethical code. As Louisa explained years later in *Transcendental Wild Oats* (1873), her fictional, light-hearted account of Fruitlands, they also refused other foods offered by kindly neighbours. 'They preached vegetarianism everywhere and resisted all temptations of the flesh, contentedly eating apples and bread at well-spread tables, and afflicting hospitable hostesses by denouncing their food.'[24]

Alcott's and Lane's beliefs were a curious combination of progressive thinking and the Puritan conviction that self-denial leads to a pure soul. But as practised at Fruitlands, their spiritual quest was doomed from the start. Neither man was prepared for the realities of living off the land. They had moved to the farmhouse in summer, too late to sow enough grain and vegetables to sustain them through the winter. Instead of working the land, Lane and Alcott spent much of their time away from the farm trying to recruit more members, while Alcott's wife, Abba, struggled to provide the basic necessities for the community. Without meat, milk, butter, eggs, wool or animal labour, Abba, the only adult female at Fruitlands, wryly noted that she was the farm's only beast of burden.[25] The young Louisa, only eleven years old at the time, kept a Fruitlands diary in which she recorded her experiences and doubts about the life her father had chosen for the family. As described by John Matteson, the author of *Eden's Outcasts* (2007), a biography of Louisa and her father, Bronson argued for the rights of all living things, 'but when worm-eaten apples arrived at the dinner table . . . she wondered whether earthly comforts were so terrible as her father made them out to be'.[26]

By December, Abba was determined to leave with her daughters. Encouraged by Lane, Alcott seriously considered staying without them, but in his struggle to decide between his family and his spiritual goals, he fell into a deep depression, refused food and nearly died. He eventually recovered and, together with his family, left Fruitlands, just seven months after its founding. In *Transcendental Wild Oats*, Louisa compares Fruitlands to the Garden of Eden, ironically noting that it was an attempt to 'plant a Paradise . . . without the possibility of a serpent moving in'.[27] At the end of the book, as the family leaves for the last time, the fictional father exclaims, '"Poor Fruitlands! The name was as great a failure as the rest!" [he] continued . . . with a sigh, as a frostbitten apple fell from a leafless bough at his feet.' His wife replies, 'Don't you think Apple Slump would be a better name for it, dear?'[28] The name, a humorous play on the traditional apple dessert that 'slumps' under its doughy covering, was one that Louisa had come up with for another Alcott home years before writing *Transcendental Wild Oats*. After leaving Fruitlands and spending several years on the edge of poverty, the Alcotts had managed to return to

Concord, Massachusetts, the centre of the Transcendentalist movement, to a home that Bronson christened Orchard House because
of the apple trees on the property. Unlike Fruitlands, this Apple
Slump would prove to be a fortunate home for the Alcotts: it was
the place where Louisa wrote the enormously successful *Little Women*
(1868–9), which ensured the family's financial future.

One of the most famous men of Alcott's day – and one who
presents a radical contrast to his lifestyle – was also a devotee of
simple food, particularly apples and bread. John D. Rockefeller (1839–
1937), the founder of Standard Oil, was one of the wealthiest men
of the Gilded Age, but, true to his Baptist upbringing, he did not
believe in indulgence and his daily diet was not much different from
Alcott's. His breakfast consisted of bread and milk, and in the evening
he ate 'a paper bag of apples'.[29] Apples also represent a wholesome
American diet in the poem 'Apple Pie and Cheese' (*A Little Book of
Western Verse*, 1889) by Eugene Field. The poet, who says he is 'loyal
to the victuals our grandsires used to eat', writes with a curious combination of American humour and xenophobia about European taste:

> Full many a sinful notion
> Conceived by foreign powers
> Has come across the ocean
> To harm this land of ours;
> And heresies called fashions
> Have modesty effaced,
> And baleful, morbid passions
> Corrupt our native taste.
> O tempora! O mores!
> What profanations these
> That seek to dim the glories
> Of apple-pie and cheese!
>   . . .
> So let the foolish choose 'em
> Of the heresy they're in;

Floris van Dyck, *Still-life with Fruit, Nuts and Cheese*, 1613, oil on canvas.

> But I, when I undress me
> Each night upon my knees
> Will ask the Lord to bless me
> With apple pie and cheese.

Apparently Field was not aware that cheese and apple pie was a combination traditionally eaten in England's West Country, known for its apples, dairy cows and Cheddar cheese.[30]

The novelist Henry James (1843–1916) also used apples to contrast Europe and America, but from a cosmopolitan's point of view. In an essay about an American artist who moved to Europe in the mid-nineteenth century and returned to the USA decades later, he was also writing about his own cultural re-entry:

> Very special and very interesting it is to catch . . . the state of being of the American who has bitten deep into the apple . . . of Europe and then has been obliged to take his lips from the fruit . . . The apple of America is a totally different apple, which, however firm and round and ruddy, is not to be . . . negotiated . . . by the same set of teeth.[31]

Returning to the USA in 1904 after nearly 30 years living abroad, James found much to criticize in this 'vast crude democracy of trade'.[32] But the beauty of the old apple orchards of New England filled him with delight and nostalgia. In *The American Scene* (1907), his memoir of his eight-month sojourn in his native land, his description of the orchards is as lyrical as Thoreau's Transcendentalist ode:

> The apple-tree, in New England, plays the part of the olive in Italy . . . What it must do for the too under-dressed land in May and June is easily supposable; but its office in the early autumn is to scatter coral and gold. The apples are everywhere and every interval, every old clearing, an orchard; they have run down from neglect and shrunken from cheapness – you pick them up from under your feet but to bite into them, for fellowship, and throw them away; but as you catch their young brightness in the blue air, where they suggest strings of strange-coloured pearls tangled in the knotted boughs, as you note their manner of swarming for a brief and wasted gaiety, they seem to ask to be praised only by the cheerful shepherd and the oaten pipe.[33]

Apple Fever

Two prominent American artists of the early twentieth century, the painter Georgia O'Keeffe and the photographer Alfred Stieglitz, also had a significant apple interlude in their creative lives. Each year from 1918 to 1934, the couple left New York City to spend the summer and autumn at Stieglitz's family estate, a former farm on Lake George in New York's Adirondack Mountains. In 1921 the old apple orchards produced a bumper crop and, as Stieglitz reported to a friend, O'Keeffe got a case of 'apple fever'.[34] Returning to figurative studies after the abstract works that had brought her fame, she produced about fifteen apple paintings, but these were a departure from traditional still-life art. To O'Keeffe, who famously said of art that 'Nothing is less real

Georgia O'Keeffe, *Apple Family III*, 1921, oil on canvas.

than realism', an apple was more than an apple.[35] The fruit in her paintings are not placed in a familiar setting, such as a garden or on a kitchen table; nor do they have realistic details. In groups and as a single apple floating on a plate, they are highly intensified portraits of reality that convey the artist's personal reaction.[36]

During the same period (1921–2), Stieglitz made a series of sixteen photographs that prominently display apples as symbols of American art and thought. Several are of O'Keeffe posing with tree branches or a large bowl of the fruit. Stieglitz had introduced her art to a wide audience in his gallery in New York City, and saw her as a true American artist drawing inspiration from her native land rather than from European art. Another photograph in the series, of the social and literary critic Waldo Frank, uses apples to convey the writer's ideas about the state of America. Frank sits on the porch of the Lake George house holding three partly eaten apples, while two half-eaten ones lie on the floor. In 1919, following the devastation of Europe during the First World War, Frank had published *Our America*, through which he believed that his generation of American artists was creating the nation's spiritual rebirth apart from its European heritage. Stieglitz's photo of Frank, which the photographer called his 'apple portrait', implies that Frank had bitten into the fruit of American experience in order to reveal America's hidden spirit.[37]

For many of the artists and writers in Stieglitz's circle, the apple was a symbol of America. The literary and music critic Paul Rosenfeld called America 'the apple laden place . . . the Earthly Paradise'.[38] But not all these symbols were positive. The poet William Carlos Williams called America 'the acrid and poisonous apple' that lay ahead of Columbus.[39] For Hart Crane, apples in the hands of an artist could become the expression of an intense creative moment. In 'Sunday Morning Apples' (1927), a poem dedicated to the painter William Sommer, he wrote:

> I have seen the apples there that toss you secrets,
> Beloved apples of seasonable madness
> That feed your inquiries with aerial wine.
> Put them beside a pitcher with a knife,
> And poise them full and ready for explosion –
> The apples, Bill, the apples!

One of the most famous American poets of the twentieth century, Robert Frost, wrote many poems about apples and was an enthusiastic apple grower in New England. Trees are a pervasive image in his poetry, and while he wrote about several different kinds, apples were a favourite. His apple poems convey the sensual experience of being in an orchard. In 'Unharvested' (*A Further Range*, 1936), he describes 'a scent of ripeness from over a wall' before finding that 'the ground was one circle of solid red'. And in one of his most famous poems, 'After Apple Picking' (*North of Boston*, 1915), he hears 'from the cellar bin/ The rumbling sound/ Of load on load of apples coming in.' In 1920 he decided to move from northern New Hampshire to southern Vermont because it offered a better climate for growing apples. Writing to a friend at the time, he said, 'I mean to plant a new Garden of Eden with a thousand apple trees of some unforbidden variety.'[40] Apple growing, he later observed, was a good occupation for a poet: 'One of my apple trees, standing stock still and rooted, earns more money in a year than I can earn with all my locomotion and artistic development.'[41] However, since writing poems and teaching left him with little time for actual farming, his son tended the apple orchard. Yet even in old age, he never tired of growing apples. At the age of 83, his response to a nurseryman about his order of apple scions for a new home in Vermont is full of anticipation: 'Your letter fills my hibernation with springtime dreams. There's nothing I like to think about more than apples.'[42]

Bigger is Better

While American Transcendentalists, artists and poets were focusing on the beauty, purity and spiritual essence of the apple, the business of growing apples in America was becoming very big indeed. It turned out that all those years of growing trees from seeds had given American apples a distinct horticultural advantage for breeders and growers – much greater genetic variety than that shown by grafted apples of the Old World. The American trees had been planted not just seed by seed. Like Johnny Appleseed, many nineteenth-century farmers had replanted the residue from cider presses, the sticky mass containing thousands of seeds in each clump. Millions of seedlings carrying infinite genetic possibilities sprouted, able to grow and establish their offspring in radically different soils and terrains in the vast American landscape. Although the science of genetics was still unknown to horticulturalists of the early twentieth century, they recognized, as S. A. Beach explained in 1905, that

> the great variability of the apple seedlings is a most valuable feature. It has made possible more rapid progress than could otherwise have been made in developing varieties especially well adapted to succeed in the new world.[43]

Endowed with this vast resource, American apple breeders eventually created the most important apple cultivars, the ones with the most recognized names on the worldwide market: Red Delicious, Golden Delicious, McIntosh and Jonathan, the source of a continuing production of successful hybrids.[44]

In the 1920s Red Delicious, Golden Delicious and other successful cultivars were planted extensively in Washington State, where the climate and soil conditions were heaven-sent for growing apples. After the Second World War, salesmen from such nurseries as Stark Brothers, the first propagator of the Red Delicious apple, began calling on farmers. It was much easier to order trees from the glossy colour catalogues than to graft them from old orchards.[45] With modern transportation and storage facilities, the big nurseries and orchards could ship trees and fruit just about anywhere. Led by Washington State, which jumped ahead of New York as the biggest apple producer in the country, the U.S. became the biggest producer of apples in the world. But the nation's lead began to slip towards the end of the twentieth century. Back in the 1920s, actors in New York City had an expression for getting their name on a Broadway marquee – 'taking a bite out of the Big Apple'. To the American apple industry today, the expression has taken on a very different meaning. Increasingly since the 1990s, growers from Australia, New Zealand, Chile, South Africa and, above all, China, have aggressively entered the market. Selling hybrids of U.S. cultivars, both in the USA and around the world, they are taking a big bite out of the American apple.

overleaf: A lavish display of apples in an unlikely place: the Bellagio Hotel and Casino in Las Vegas, 2007.

Lucas Cranach the Elder, *The Virgin and Child under an Apple Tree*, 1520—26.
The apple in the infant's hand symbolizes the promise of man's redemption for
original sin. The crust of bread in his other hand represents the body of Christ.

six

Apple Adulation

A s the apple migrated from the forests of Central Asia across Europe and reached North America, it was embraced by Western cultures, perhaps more than any other edible plant. Like its cousin the rose, the apple was imbued with emotional power in mythology and religion. It also took hold in agriculture, the arts and the aphorisms of daily life. The many biblical references to the apple, in the Garden of Eden and in several famous sayings such as 'Comfort me with apples' from the Song of Songs (also known as the Song of Solomon), are among the best-known apple stories and adages. Many scholars believe that these passages probably refer to other fruits more likely to grow in the Middle Eastern climate, but – like the lily of the Old and New Testaments, which botanists claim could be any number of flowers – the apple of the Bible became the image we know so well today. It was burned into the public mind centuries ago by countless paintings that portray the Garden of Eden at that fateful moment when Eve offers Adam what is unmistakably an apple, often a tempting red one.

One of the most memorable images of the apple is in *Adam and Eve* (1526) by the German Renaissance painter Lucas Cranach the Elder, a supporter of Martin Luther's reformist campaign and a stern believer in the Bible. Portrayed moments before the Fall, the garden in his painting is a true paradise, with perfectly round, bright-red apples hanging from every branch of the Tree of Knowledge. Cranach also depicted apples prominently in several paintings of the Madonna and Child, including *Madonna under the Apple Tree* (*c.* 1525) and *Virgin and Child under an Apple Tree* (*c.* 1530).

Apples also appear as symbols in much earlier examples of Christian art. An early wall painting (*c.* 1270–1300) in Westminster Abbey of St Christopher carrying the Christ Child departs from the usual image of this famous tale. Instead of holding an orb with a cross on top,

Netherlandish School, *The Holy Family in a Garden, c.* 1495–1505, hand-coloured woodcut. Unlike the sinful fruit of the Garden of Eden, the apples here are a bountiful presence in a peaceful scene of family life.

representing the world that weighed so heavily on the saint's shoulders, the Christ Child holds an apple – another symbol of the world's sins derived from the story of the Garden of Eden.[1] Apples are also a symbol of the Christian promise of redemption in a number of early Renaissance paintings and sculptures of the Virgin and Child. *The Madonna of Seeon*, a painted wooden statue (*c.* 1450) in Seeon Abbey in Bavaria, depicts the Virgin with one arm around the Child and the other outstretched, holding a red apple. *Our Lady of the Apple*, an earthenware sculpture (*c.* 1440–82) by Luca della Robbia, portrays the Child grasping the apple. The painting *Christ and John the Baptist as Children* (*c.* 1655–60) by Bartolomé Murillo is a vision of innocence with golden apples strewn at the feet of the embracing toddlers.

Treasured Sweets

Many places where apples grew took some form of the name of the fruit, from Almaty ('father of apples') in Kazakhstan to countless Appletons, Applefords and Applebys in Britain and North America. While Roman horticulture died in the chaos of the invasions, the Angle-Jute-Saxon invaders left the apple names behind, usually as a prefix in the names of villages and small towns in Britain, such as Apley, Appleby, Appledore and Appleford.[2] The names suggest that these places were relics of sweet-apple orchards planted by the Romans and treasured by later owners. The legend of the Isle of Avalon is also most likely derived from a place where sweet apples grew. Their taste was treasured throughout history at times when sugar was unavailable or in short supply.

Many eighteenth-century American homesteaders planted apple orchards before they began to build their homes. Planting with seeds meant that it was some time before they could savour the fruits of their labour, but as one settler of Ohio in 1800 noted, the wait was well worth it. Like most struggling farmers of the period, his family lived on whatever they could coax out of the land. Turnips and wild nuts were staples. Peach trees produced fruit from seedlings much

Apple picking scene on a quartz box mounted in gold and encrusted with jewels,
c. 1765, Dresden. The apples are made from garnets, carnelians and pink sapphires.

sooner than apple trees did, and provided a welcome taste of sweetness. Apples were a greater treat: 'We got a bushel of apples for each day's work in picking peaches. These were kept for particular eating as if they had contained seeds of gold.'[3]

When sugar became more widely available, apples baked as desserts tasted even sweeter and more tempting, particularly to the English palate. In the eighteenth century, when Britain's plantations in the West Indies made sugar plentiful and affordable, apple desserts were all the rage.[4] Puddings, pies, tarts and custards had been a mainstay of British cookery for centuries, but cooks in many more households were now able to indulge the English sweet tooth with innovative preparations of sweetened fruit in pastry, pancakes, dumplings, fritters and other culinary creations. One dish, made of a light sponge mixture of eggs, sugar and flour poured on top of apples and baked, was known as Eve's Pudding.[5] Topped with beaten egg whites, it became Apple Snow. Victorians who had become wealthy through the sugar trade enjoyed elaborate desserts, such as Apples à la Portugaise, a pastry filled with apple marmalade, topped with a dome of sliced apples and covered with meringue. After baking, it was decorated with stripes of redcurrant and apple jelly.[6] English culinary apples, firm and not too sweet, were the preferred fruit for baked desserts, as amusingly described by the connoisseur Edward Bunyard in 1937: 'The best English apples by long training know how to behave in a pie; they melt but do not squelch; they inform but do not dominate.'[7] It is no wonder that cooking apples are still a market favourite in England.

Apple Comrades

Although they would not have agreed on anything else, Thomas Jefferson, Queen Charlotte and Vladimir Lenin shared a love of tasty apples. Jefferson was a connoisseur of fine apples, but, like most Americans, he thought the ones from home were the best. Serving as minister to France in the 1780s and presumably enjoying sumptuous French food, he complained in a letter from Paris to a friend back home: 'They have no apples here to compare with our Newtown Pippin.'[8] Jefferson's contemporary Queen Charlotte (1744–1818), the wife of America's Revolutionary War nemesis George III, was a horticultural enthusiast and lent her name to several new varieties of apple. Notably stout of figure, she is remembered most of all for the dish Apple Charlotte. This traditional British pudding, usually made with Bramley apples, sugar, butter, marmalade and stale bread, is said to have been the creation of the famous French chef Marie-Antoine Carême, who served the Prince Regent during George III's mental illness and named the dessert in the queen's honour. The father of Russian communism, meanwhile, shared the queen's love of apple desserts and might even have approved of the use of stale bread. But, despite his ideological frugality, Lenin preferred his apples in cake, not bread. As the Russian-born food writer Anya von Bremzen recalls in her memoir about growing up in the Soviet era of the 1960s, 'all Soviet children knew of Lenin's fondness for apple cake.' Yet, as she explains further, the story of his love of apples is soured by Soviet moralism:

Sorting apples on a boat at the market on the banks of the Seine, Paris, 1908.

Even more, we knew how child-Lenin once secretly gob-
bled up the apple peels after his mom baked such a cake.
But the future leader owned up to his crime. He bravely
confessed it to his mother! This was the moral. We all had
to grow up honest like Lenin.[9]

The story is similar to another morality tale based on a fruit tree,
one all American children know well: how the young George
Washington chopped down his father's cherry tree and afterwards
confessed, 'Father, I cannot tell a lie, I cut down the tree.' Both
stories became national myths, revealing more about the culture of
their times than about actual events. Washington's was popularized
in the nineteenth century as a parable of honesty and humility.
Although Lenin's tale conveys the same message, the apple peelings
are a telling sign of harsh reality. In most countries where fruit was
widely available, the story of a child secretly gobbling up apple peel
would be surprising, even for Lenin, who grew up in a comfortable
household. But during the Soviet era of food shortages, even the
peel of the apple was coveted.

Apple Rivals

American claims to producing the best apples, such as those put forth by Henry Ward Beecher in the late nineteenth century, roused a similar cry in Britain. Besieged by imported apples from America, France and their Commonwealth countrymen in Canada, Australia, New Zealand and South Africa, English growers of the late nineteenth and early twentieth centuries found themselves at a terrible disadvantage. English apples, mostly grown at this time on small farms and country estates, did not look as perfect or keep for as long as the imports, and even if English growers wanted to follow the lead of the bigger commercial operations, they were stymied by the cool, wet English climate, which was inhospitable to the new cultivars. Like their rivals in America, the English responded with patriotic claims for their native apples, adding jibes directed at their biggest competitor: 'The public will soon learn to discriminate between the brightly coloured but dry and flavourless American kinds and fresh home grown apples', a nurseryman wrote in 1881.[10] He and other horticulturalists urged English growers to focus on their best varieties and promote them to the English public.

In the coming decades, bursts of apple mania broke out on both sides of the Atlantic. Trying to catch up with their better-organized rivals, English specialists from groups such as the Royal Horticultural Society (RHS) and the Worshipful Company of Fruiterers embarked on a national fruit crusade. They drummed up support from every county to document a complete collection of English varieties and showcased them in a series of national exhibitions, beginning with the National Apple Congress of 1883. More than 1,500 varieties were set out at the RHS gardens in a triumphant display that, according to a report from a horticultural journal of the day, 'had to be kept open for an extra week to accommodate all those who wanted to see it'.[11]

British apple orchards increased in size and sales, but U.S. apple production kept pulling ahead and the industry enlisted everyone it could in its marketing campaigns. Photographs from the 1920s show

National Apple Week at a Washington State orphanage, 1925. The booming
American apple industry used every means to promote apples.

National Apple Week at Walter Reed Military Hospital, Washington, DC, 1925.

Apple Monument, Cornelia, Georgia, 1936. Built in 1925, the giant apple monument celebrated Cornelia's new apple industry, which saved the town from bankruptcy after its traditional cotton crops had failed.

First World War veterans in wheelchairs and children in orphanages posing with banners and bushels of apples. In Washington State's Yakima Valley, the heart of its apple industry, bakers gathered to prepare 'the world's largest apple pie', with 400 gallons of apples in a pan 3 m (10 ft) wide. (The tradition continues today in Paradise, California.) It was all part of National Apple Week, which was created and organized by apple growers to promote their products throughout the country. After their cotton crops were destroyed by boll weevil infestations in the early 1920s, farmers in the state of Georgia switched to apples and were so thrilled with their success that they installed a giant apple monument in 1925 in the town of Cornelia. Some 2 m (7 ft) tall and nearly 7 m (22 ft) around, the painted steel and concrete apple soars even higher on its 2.5 m (8 ft) pedestal. Although apples are no longer a major crop, the town is still known as the 'Home of the Big Red Apple'.

While English apple growers today readily admit that their climate prevents them from growing most of the American varieties, many, like those in the nineteenth century, believe that they produce quality rather than quantity. English Apples & Pears, an association of growers organized in 1990, maintains that

> the absence of extreme temperatures but adequate rainfall allows our apples to grow relatively slowly and to develop their full flavour . . . those which are grown in the UK have unrivalled taste and flavour.[12]

'No fruit is more to the English taste than the apple', Edward Bunyard wrote in 1929 – and, no doubt, he would have gladly challenged Thomas Jefferson on the merits of the Newtown Pippin: 'Alas! With us it fails to produce its subtler refinements. Can it be that we lack the Puritan austerity?'[13]

Apples are Us

Before the age of corporate branding, many apple cultivators bestowed their own names on their creations, closely identifying with their namesakes. The omnipresent McIntosh bears the name of John McIntosh, who discovered it as a seedling in 1811 on his farm in Ontario, Canada. Unlike Mr McIntosh, his apples are so well known that most people today call them by their familiar nickname, 'Macs'. Theories about the famous Jonathan apple include stories of its early nineteenth-century origin in several parts of the USA. But whether or not it was named for Jonathan Higley of Ohio, Jonathan Hasbrouck of New York or some other apple grower, that person was clearly a Jonathan. One of England's most famous dessert apples, Cox's Orange Pippin, was first grown in 1825 by Richard Cox, a Buckinghamshire brewer and horticulturalist whose name lives on in the apple's several offshoots, Cherry Cox, Crimson Cox and Queen Cox. Granny Smith, the best-known Australian apple, was propagated in the mid-nineteenth century by Maria Ann Smith, known in her old age as 'Granny'. Although a series of later growers made it famous, Granny's name stuck. This was not the case with the Ben Davis apple, named for a Kentucky man who first grew it in the early nineteenth century. Like the Baldwin and many other less fortunate namesakes, such as Harrison's (a favourite American cider apple), it was forced out of the market by more successful varieties.

Family names for apples began to wane in the late nineteenth century after the Stark Brothers nursery of Missouri came upon its most famous apple. At a competition held in 1893, Clarence Stark, hoping to replace the poorly performing Ben Davis apple, tasted one called Hawkeye, submitted by a grower in Iowa. Stark was so impressed that he bought the rights to it and gave it a name he had been saving for the perfect recipient – Delicious. He promoted it as Stark's Delicious, but eventually dropped his own name after securing the rights to a West Virginia apple that he called Golden Delicious. Stark's Delicious became Red Delicious, inspiring a new generation of apples, such as Winesap, Honeycrisp (Honeycrunch) and King Luscious, that blow their own trumpets.

Before its transformation into a uniformly red orb, the Red Delicious, originally Hawkeye, had a red blush base streaked with yellow. The complex colours of nineteenth-century apples, unmatched by those of other fruits, attracted many artists and writers who saw the fruit's 'complexion' as something nearly human. 'The apple . . . should be regarded,' one writer maintained, 'not only of all fruits, but also of all flowers, as the most pleasing object to the eye, on account of the striking resemblance of its contour to the human cheek.'[14] Henry Thoreau, who felt a close affinity with the natural world, described the apple's varying colour as a reflection of the 'face of Nature'.[15] In his book *Apples and Madonnas* (1930), C. J. Bulliet, a passionate admirer of Modernism, maintained that Cézanne's apples were more expressive than the human portraits painted by a Renaissance master: 'Cézanne's apples, expressed with an elemental force akin to the forces of nature – crude and rugged – that bring apples into being, are superior to the heads of Raphael's Madonnas.'[16] In *Paul Cézanne* (1988), the eminent art historian Meyer Schapiro also described one of the artist's most famous apple paintings, *Still-life with Basket of Apples* (1890–94), as an

Paul Cézanne, *Apples and Oranges* (*Pommes et oranges*), c. 1899.

achievement comparable to a human portrait: 'The thirty or more apples, irreducibly complex in the sequence of colors, each fruit a singular piece of painting, a unique object.'[17]

The apple itself has been an art form for centuries in Japan. This highly unusual craft involves a level of painstaking care similar to that dedicated by the Japanese to the creation of bonsai, and produces artful apples that are larger, more perfect and more uniquely coloured than any other fruit. Developed in the nineteenth century and still performed today, the process begins with farmers thinning apple blossoms on the tree, from an average of 4,000 on each tree to as few as 200, leaving only the central bloom of each remaining cluster of flowers. As soon as the fruits appear, the farmer covers each with a two-layered bag, pleating it to leave room for the fruit, which can be 30 per cent larger than the average apple, to grow. Wired shut, the bags stay on for three months or more to block out sunlight and keep the apple creamy white. The opaque outer layer of the bag is then removed, leaving a translucent waxed paper cover. Depending on its colour – red, green, light or dark blue – the waxed paper will affect the fruit's ultimate colour. It is removed after about ten days, and farmers then take an exorbitant number of steps to increase the sunlight reaching each apple, trimming branches, stripping leaves, laying reflective mats on the ground to colour the bottom of the fruit, and turning each one several times to attain uniform colouring. Turning the apples without breaking their stems is a tricky business, achieved by wrapping a rubber band around each stem and looping it on to a nearby branch. For the final mark of beauty, a stencil is applied during the period of sun exposure to create a design or greeting

Bonsai apple tree.

on the skin. One Japanese pop star had stencils of his face applied to the skin to create personalized gifts. All this work requires the farmers to make countless trips up and down ladders. But the results, said to be delicious as well as beautiful, command a premium as gourmet art. Placed in an elaborate box, such a work of apple art can fetch as much as $150.[18]

Tree Tributes

Even without fruit, the apple tree itself has long been regarded as a thing of beauty, one of the few fruit trees to draw high praise when flowering and fully grown. The early sixteenth-century Mughal emperor Babur, a poet and patron of the arts, had elaborate gardens of fruit trees in Central Asia and wrote in his journal of one apple

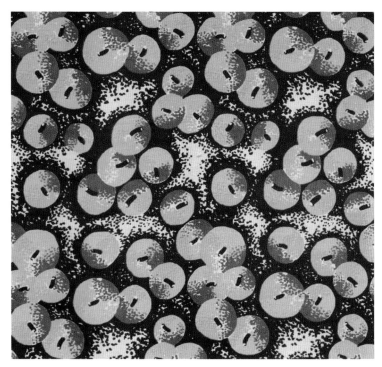

Silk fabric printed with groups of apples. Stehli Silks Corporation, c. 1930. Apples have inspired designers to reproduce the familiar image in a variety of new forms.

tree so beautiful that 'no painter trying to depict it could have equalled [it].'[19] The English art critic John Ruskin considered apple blossom to have a 'separate queendom' from common flowers, and inspired 'apple-blossom fever' among a host of painters in the mid-nineteenth century after he proclaimed:

> I believe the most beautiful position in which flowers can possibly be seen is precisely their most natural one . . . tree blossoms relieved against the sky. How it happens that no flower-painter has yet been moved to draw a cluster of boughs of . . . apple blossom, just as they grow, with the deep blue sky between every bud and petal, is more than I can understand.[20]

Other writers of the nineteenth century also marvelled at the beauty of apple blossoms. 'In May, the very flower month of the year, the crown and glory of all is the apple tree', said Beecher.[21] Even the more philosophical Ralph Waldo Emerson waxed poetic on the subject: 'The American sun paints himself in these glowing balls amid green leaves.'[22]

During the Second World War, blossoming apple trees evoked a sense of longing for home as American soldiers listened to the Andrew Sisters' recording of 'Apple Blossom Time' in 1941. The song was written in 1920, but the lyric 'I'll be seeing you in apple blossom time' became a refrain of hope during the war years. Crab-apple trees, scorned during the American war against cider and dismissed as an eating apple because of their small, bitter fruits, are now extensively cultivated for their beautiful blossom. With 800 known cultivars and new selections added yearly, they are the dominant spring-flowering tree of North America.[23]

Apple trees are also revered for their age and size, and thus evoke a sense of the past. At the start of the twentieth century, a time when dwarf trees were becoming more common in the orchards of New York, S. A. Beach observed:

MALUS BACCATA *flore roseo pleno.*

Plein air

Malus baccata (Siberian crab apple) in a botanical print of 1845.
Crab apple trees produce a profusion of blossom, which provides both
beauty and ample supplies of pollen for other trees in an orchard.

Old apple trees, like this one in New York State
in the early 20th century, evoke a sense of the past.

The old trees, having outlived their companions, stand as
silent reminders of the days of the stage-coach, the hand-
loom, the spinning-wheel, and the paring-bee, and of the
time when the farmer generally considered his winter
supplies incomplete unless there were several barrels of
cider stored in the cellar.[24]

Statuesque survivors that stood out on old farms were a favourite
subject of genre painters. Many eighteenth- and nineteenth-century
paintings depict huge trees with boys perched on sturdy limbs under
a broad umbrella of twiggy branches, pelting one another with apples
or tossing the fruit down to girls below. In the industrialized world
of the late nineteenth century, many of these scenes expressed a
profound nostalgia for country bowers of unpruned apple trees.[25]

Some apple trees seem to live forever, rejuvenating themselves
in new generations. One such tree, known as Seek-No-Further, a
name bestowed on it for its delicious fruit, was planted on top of a

mountain in Westfield, Massachusetts, in the 1700s. While the original trunk, more than 1 m (3 ft) around, fell over, some of its branches took root, and they continued to grow down the mountain over the next two centuries. As Eric Sloane describes, the tree became a symbol of human regeneration:

> As the fallen trunk decayed, new apple saplings had rooted all around it, giving the appearance of a family gathered around a dead giant on his bier. The old tree had dug its branches like fingers into the earth, a strange and striking sequence of resurrection.[26]

Venerable apple trees have also become historic monuments. One of the oldest and most famous, an apple tree in Sir Isaac Newton's seventeenth-century garden in Lincolnshire, is purported to be the one he sat under when an apple fell on his head, triggering his concept of gravity in about 1665. The tree still lives, although visitors to his historic home can no longer sit under it because the roots are threatened by the compaction of the soil, trampled by thousands who have come to see the fabled tree over years past.[27] Newton's 'Eureka' moment about gravity may not have happened precisely when an apple from this tree, a rare Flower of Kent (a green cooking apple), fell on his head. But the story gathered so much steam over the years that the tree, or rather a 10 cm (4 in.) piece of its wood, actually took off into space in 2010. Placed on board the space shuttle *Atlantis* to commemorate the Royal Society's 350th anniversary, it would have amazed Newton by defying gravity.[28]

Another famous English tree, the original Bramley apple tree, has a more down-to-earth history, yet one that is equally relished in the UK. The forebear of Britain's famous cooking apple, it is more than 200 years old and still produces generous crops of apples in the Nottinghamshire cottage garden where it began. Planted as a chance seedling by a young girl in 1809, it was nurtured by the next resident of the cottage, Matthew Bramley, who allowed a local nurseryman

In this satirical cover of *Puck* magazine, 1910, Sir Isaac Newton discovers the theory of gravity when a Wright Brothers plane crashes onto his apple tree.

to take cuttings and sell the fruit, as long as it would bear the Bramley name. The original tree was blown down in a violent storm in 1900, but miraculously survived and continues to bear fruit.[29]

The progenitor of America's famous Baldwin apple, however, is long gone, felled by a gale in 1815. The fruit was originally called Woodpecker because the birds liked the old tree, and probably contributed to its decline. It was renamed in honour of Colonel Loammi Baldwin (1744–1807), a Massachusetts engineer and veteran of the Revolutionary War, who first propagated the apple from scions of the original tree. The spot in Wilmington, Massachusetts, where the tree is believed to have sprouted as a chance seedling is marked by a granite apple on a 1.8 m (6 ft) pedestal, erected by the local historical society in 1895 on a site known as the Garden of Eden.[30] The stone apple is much smaller than the 'Big Red Apple' of Georgia, but both monuments commemorate the old days of small-town apple industries.

One of the earliest and most unusual tributes to the apple tree is the centuries-old English tradition of wassailing or singing to the tree on Twelfth Night. The practice, which differed somewhat from county to county in cider-producing areas, was a jolly affair of drinking and toasting the trees with a mixture of cider and ale. Twelfth Night falls after the winter solstice, and the revellers would make a great deal of noise, presumably to wake the trees from their winter sleep. Unlike the more familiar Christmas tradition of wassailing carols, wassailing the trees began as a superstitious ritual to ensure a good apple harvest for the next season, and often included elements of religious ceremony. Neighbours and family members, including small children, would go from orchard to orchard, sprinkling trees with cider or leaving a jug of cider and pieces of cider-soaked toast in the branches of the biggest tree as an offering to the apple-tree gods.[31] A small boy might be lifted on to a branch and fed pieces of the cider toast – a ritual possibly derived from Arthurian legend. In one of those twelfth-century tales of the search for the Holy Grail, knight Perceval comes upon the Christ Child in a tree, an element that also links the wassailing of trees to the Christmas season. But it could also have deeper roots in pre-Christian ceremonies, possibly in Roman tributes to Pomona, the goddess of fruit and gardens. However, a poem published in London's *Spiritual Magazine* in 1761, 'Jesus Christ the Apple Tree', erases any thoughts of pagan influences on the apple tree:

This fruit does make my soul to thrive
It keeps my dying faith alive
Which makes my soul in haste to be
With Jesus Christ the apple tree.[32]

Set to music by a number of composers, it became a familiar American hymn and is still performed during the Christmas season. Although the hymn might have been an effort to Christianize wassailing, the tradition has not died. Whether it is a relic of sacrifice to Pomona, a tribute to the Christ Child, or simply an excuse for having a drink, apple-tree wassailing is having a revival of sorts today in Britain and America. In some places, it takes place not on Twelfth Night but on a more convenient pre-Christmas date, making wassailing festivals a good way for orchards to attract holiday shoppers. Some orchards postpone the wassailing until spring, when the trees are in bloom and the weather is more attractive to customers.

Thoreau would be happy to know that wild apple trees growing in forests also have their champions today. All fruit trees need sunshine to produce fruit, but apple trees grown on old fields that have been reforested are dying out because they have been overshadowed by larger trees. Since many forms of wildlife depend upon wild apples for food and habitat, the Natural Resources Conservation Service of the U.S. Department of Agriculture has begun an 'apple release program' to cut the branches from trees that are shading and crowding out apples.[33]

Charles Hazelwood Shannon, *Autumn*, 1917, lithograph.

seven

Good Apples

From ancient mythology to modern marketing campaigns, the apple has been a symbol of nearly every good thing that man could want: an earthly paradise, youth, love, immortality and, if not everlasting life, at least wholesome food and good health. As in the Garden of Eden, the apple of many mythological tales is a tempting fruit, but one unspoiled by sin. In the ancient Greek Garden of the Hesperides, the golden apples were the source of immortality. Although Hercules steals them from the hundred-headed dragon guarding the tree, this fierce reptile, unlike the serpent in the Garden of Eden, does not cause the Fall of man. In the *Prose Edda*, the thirteenth-century book of Norse legends, Idun, the goddess of spring, is the keeper of the apples of immortality, which the gods eat to preserve their youth. The composer Richard Wagner wove her story into *Das Rheingold*, the prologue to his four-part opera *Der Ring des Nibelungen*, merging Idun's tale with that of Freia, the Germanic goddess of love, youth and beauty. Botticelli's joyful painting *Primavera* (*c.* 1482) depicts the Roman gods Venus, Cupid, Flora and Mercury celebrating spring as the season of love and new life as they frolic under a bower of trees laden with apples.

The biblical sayings 'Comfort me with apples' and 'apple of my eye' also allude to the theme of love. The full saying, 'Comfort me with apples for I am sick with love', suggests apples as an antidote to passion. But in the folk traditions of many apple-growing countries, an apple or even just its peel or seeds could be used to predict

Edward Burne-Jones, *The Garden of the Hesperides*, tempera and gilt painting, 1882. In this representation of the classical myth, the daughters of Hesperus tend the dragon guarding the golden apples of Hera. Although Hercules steals the apples, the fierce reptile, unlike the serpent in the Garden of Eden, does not cause the fall of man.

Silver pomander shaped as an apple, *c.* 1350, Italy, possibly a love token worn hanging from a chain at a woman's waist.

Krishna visiting Radha, watercolour, *c.* 1695, India. Radha, the feminine aspect of God in Hinduism, awaits Krishna, the masculine figure. She sits in a pavilion inside of which are three alcoves containing apples, symbols of her love.

partners in love and marriage. A common ritual was to twirl a piece of apple peel around one's head and then toss it to the ground, where it would supposedly form the first letter of a true love's name. Another was to heat apple seeds in a pan to find out, as in plucking the petals of a daisy, if a loved one 'loves me or loves me not'. If a seed popped after one asked the question, love was on the way. Myths and folklore also portray apples as symbols and even a source of fertility. In Kyrgyzstan, for example, it was said that a woman having difficulty becoming pregnant should roll on the ground beneath an apple tree, in the hope that some of its ability to bear fruit would rub off on her.[1]

Wholesomeness and innocence are evident in eighteenth- and nineteenth-century genre paintings of mothers and children picking apples and of rosy, apple-cheeked children eating or bobbing for apples. An apple also became a symbol of fatherly devotion in the age-old tale of a father shooting an apple off the head of his son. A motif of German and Scandinavian folklore, the story became well

F. W. Edmonds, *Sparking*, 1839, print. The man in this American
scene gazes lovingly at the woman as she peels apples.

Farmer beating down apples as children collect them below, Normandy, *c.* 1900.

William Tell, 1774, etching. In this German folk tale, the father, forced to shoot an
apple off his son's head, proves both his marksmanship and his devotion to his son.

known in *William Tell*, the play of 1804 by Friedrich Schiller and
subsequent opera by Rossini (1829). Tell is arrested for failing to
show respect to a cruel Austrian overlord. As punishment, the overlord
forces Tell to shoot the apple off the head of his son with a single
shot from his crossbow, and warns that, should he fail, both father
and son will be put to death. After splitting the apple, Tell reveals
that he had brought along additional arrows to kill the overlord, had
the first shot failed. He later murders the overlord as revenge for
endangering the life of his son. Rossini's opera emphasizes the father's
love for his son and broadens the theme into a successful peasant
revolt against a tyrant.

Apples embody the innocence of childhood, as in the schoolhouse
phrases 'an apple for the teacher' and 'A is for Apple.' They also
suggest tidiness, as in 'apple-pie order', and the reverse, as in 'upsetting
the applecart'. Kate Greenaway's book *A Apple Pie* (1886) illustrates
the entire alphabet with apple-pie vignettes: 'A was an apple pie; B
bit it; C cut it; D dealt it; F fought for it', and so on.

Baby cupid shooting an apple off a woman's head, photo, c. early 20th century.
A humorous twist on the William Tell story.

'A was a lovely apple', pen and ink drawing from *Nonsense Alphabet* by Edward Lear (c. 1880). Apples in children's books often embody the innocence of childhood.

Upsetting the applecart, photo. c. 1903; children enact the old saying.

'Tis a pie, Your Majesty', he said simply, 'an apple pie.' Illustration
from 'The King's Pie', by Abbie Farwell Brown in a 1911 issue
of *St Nicholas Magazine*. In this tale of a baker who presents an apple
pie to a king, apples, like virtue, prove to be their own reward.

In some children's stories, apples, like virtue, prove to be their
own reward. 'The King's Pie', a story published in 1911 in a popular
American children's magazine, tells the tale of a poor young baker,
a virtuous man who feeds the poor and also tries to prepare a pie
fit for a king. This was a time, the narrator explains, when 'there
was no such thing known as a pie made of fruit'; pies were only 'meat
of some sort baked in a dish covered with dough', and were 'vulgar,
ordinary victuals'. In preparation for the king's visit, the pretentious
Lord Mayor invites the town's master chefs to compete in preparing
a 'great, glorified, poetic, pie'. The chef who wins the king's approval
is to receive 'a team of white oxen; a hundred sacks of white flour;
and a hundred pieces of white silver'. While the cooks prepare fan-
tastically elaborate pies – including one that bursts open with singing
children – the poor baker, using just a little flour, butter and sugar,
and apples from his only tree, prepares a simple but delicious pie.
The king gobbles it up with relish and declares that the poor baker
will henceforth be known as Baron Applepy. He lives happily ever

after, using his prize money and sacks of flour to feed the poor people of the town.[2]

Good for You

The slogan 'An apple a day keeps the doctor away' was first recorded in 1904, and is said to be an adaptation of the old English proverb 'An apple before going to bed keeps the doctor from earning his bread.' But apples have been considered healthy for much longer even than that. The second-century Roman physician Galen recommended them as part of a good diet.[3] By his time, Romans had been cultivating sweet apples for centuries, replacing the sour fruit that often caused stomach distress. Apples are also a traditional part of the Jewish celebration of Rosh Hashanah, eaten as a wish for 'a sweet new year'.

Today's claims for the apple go far beyond all these beliefs. A number of studies, including several funded by the American apple industry, have indicated that it is a veritable superfruit, one that can reduce cholesterol and weight, help prevent many types of cancer, stroke and dementia, and, as a result, lengthen the life. In 2005 Washington State apple growers, in partnership with a national chain of gyms, promoted a new diet book, *The Three-apple-a-day Plan: Your Foundation for Permanent Fat Loss.* The gyms launched a 'Get-in-Shape' contest and encouraged participants to eat an apple before each meal, a sure way to curb one's appetite.[4]

Apple industry websites list many other benefits of eating apples, most commonly that they are 'a significant source of Vitamin C'. Other sources point out that oranges, a more popular fruit in volumes of worldwide consumption, contain much more vitamin C. But the latest thinking on nutrition emphasizes that the apple's benefits are greater than a single vitamin. Packed with plant-based nutrients (phytonutrients) and natural chemicals (phytochemicals), plus fibre and a host of other elements that can keep you healthy, the apple, according to this way of thinking, is much greater than the sum of

Swiss poster, c. 1930s, promoting apples and milk as part of
'the fight against alcohol' which, in turn, 'promotes public security'.

its parts. 'It is now clear', according to the nutritional scientist T. Colin Campbell, 'that there are hundreds if not thousands of chemicals in apples, each of which, in turn, may affect thousands of reactions and metabolic systems'.[5] Nutritionists particularly recommend eating the apple with its skin, which is rich in phytonutrients, containing 50 per cent more than in a peeled apple.[6] Unfortunately, the skin is also the source of pesticides in apples that have been sprayed.

But not all apples have the same nutrients. Henry Thoreau may not have realized it, but his preference for wild rather than cultivated apples was far and above the healthiest choice. Wild apples, even bitter crab apples, are 'vastly more nutritious than our cultivated varieties', according to the food writer Jo Robinson. She points to a U.S. Department of Agriculture survey conducted in 2003 of 321 wild and domesticated apples, showing that the wild species have '475 times more phytonutrients . . . Throughout our long history of cultivating apples,' she maintains, 'we have squandered a wealth of nutrients.'[7] The old standard Golden Delicious, one of the world's most popular apples, along with some of the newest, sweetest varieties, such as Fuji and Ginger Gold, barely registered on the USDA's phytonutrient scale. But there is no need to give up eating sweet apples. While sour crab apples will never tempt our sugar-spoiled palates, there are many healthy options in today's markets. Robinson lists the following, based on the USDA survey, as the most nutritious of the supermarket varieties: Braeburn, Cortland, Discovery, Gala, Granny Smith, Honeycrisp (Honeycrunch), Idared, McIntosh, Melrose, Ozark Gold and Red Delicious.[8]

Some studies indicate that seedling and heirloom apples have great anti-cancer properties. One variety, called Monty's Surprise, discovered on an old tree in New Zealand in 2000, revealed unusually strong cancer-fighting potential in laboratory tests, as well as great flavour and a plethora of phytonutrients. The man who discovered it, Mark Christensen, has donated more than 8,000 trees of the variety to New Zealanders.[9] Even the sweetest apples are a much better snack than a sweet or chocolate bar. While sweets cause blood-sugar levels to spike, the fibre in the apple slows down the absorption of sugar into the bloodstream.

Redder is Better – Or is It?

Despite the many green and yellow varieties, red is the colour we most associate with apples, and the one favoured by many growers who go to great lengths to make their fruit the reddest of them all. Reflective sheets are sometimes laid between trees to increase sunlight, which generates riper and redder apples. Computer software has been developed to measure the redness, and, most recently, genetic analysis has identified the gene that produces the red colour – a discovery that could lead to new genetic breeding and more red apples.[10] Seeing red is a healthy option according to Robinson, who says that the reddest apples have the most nutrients because they have been exposed to the most sun, usually through extensive pruning of branches.[11]

But is redder truly better? In 2011 scientists studying whether or not eating deeply coloured fruit and vegetables reduced the risk of strokes found that red apples were no better than yellow or green ones.[12] All were equally good at lowering the risk. And redness often comes at the expense of taste. Taste tests of strains of Red Delicious apples have found that 'the more perfectly red the apple, the more bland and insipid its flavor.'[13] Apples that redden early are sometimes picked prematurely so that they will keep for longer, and this can have a devastating effect on their flavour. The redder they are, the more they disguise bruising – another fact that helps the sale of more red apples. After hearing the redder-is-better claim, the orchardist Ezekiel Goodband, who raises heirlooms of many different colours, replied half-jokingly, 'That's pomological profiling.'[14] Robinson readily admits that green- or yellow-skinned varieties that do not turn red with sun exposure are also a healthy choice, although it is difficult to judge their ripeness. In any case, the all-green Granny Smith apples 'have more phytonutrients than many of the reddest apples,' she says, 'so they are always a good choice'.[15]

The apple most often depicted as New York City's Big Apple is red, but a coalition of environmental groups has campaigned to make it green. It would celebrate the historic Newtown Pippin, although people in Virginia might complain, since that variety, which they call the Albemarle Pippin, has been grown there for hundreds of years. All the same, the New York groups argue, a green apple would be an appropriate symbol for a city trying to be environmentally green.[16]

Adam and Eve in America, print from *A briefe and true report of the new found land of Virginia*, drawn by Theodor de Bry, 1590. Eve is not the only guilty female in this depiction. Even the serpent has the head and upper body of a woman.

eight

Bad Apples

༄

Calling someone a 'bad apple' labels him or her as a person with evil at the core, and, like that one bad apple in the barrel, someone with a corrupting influence on others. The apple itself, of course, is not to blame for all the bad things it has been made to represent. It seems quite unfair that we do not berate the peach or the plum or any other fruit that spoils more quickly than the hardy apple. But mushy bananas and soggy strawberries are not the stuff of poetry. On the contrary, the omnipresent apple has an insidious fault that is ripe for literary picking. Its tendency to rot slowly and invisibly from the inside lends itself to many wicked themes. Whatever the cause – ethylene gas or maggots – a rotten apple is an apt symbol of hidden evil. Shakespeare used the image most memorably in *The Merchant of Venice* (Act I, Scene iii), when Antonio speaks of Shylock's proposal for loaning money:

> The devil can cite Scripture for his purpose.
> An evil soul producing holy witness
> Is like a villain with a smiling cheek,
> A goodly apple rotten at the heart:
> O, what a goodly outside falsehood hath!

Shakespeare also used the metaphor in Sonnet 93 to convey a sense of falseness masquerading as beauty. The voice is that of a lover who adores the face of his beloved yet suspects her of unfaithfulness: 'How

Two apples, one fresh and one rotten. Although the rotten apple is obvious in this photo, the apple's tendency to rot invisibly from the inside has become a literary metaphor for hidden evil.

like Eve's apple doth thy beauty grow,/ If thy sweet virtue answer not thy show.'

Sinful Apples

'Eve's apple' brings us to the source of the quintessential bad apple, the fruit of the Garden of Eden, forever imprinted in Western culture as the embodiment of temptation and sin. In his ode to wild apples, Henry Thoreau glides over their sinful role in the Garden of Eden: 'Some have thought that the first human pair were tempted by its fruit.'[1] Yet it is Eve – and all women portrayed ever after as temptresses – who bears the brunt of the blame. In Lucas Cranach the Elder's *Adam and Eve* (1526), Adam innocently scratches his head as he accepts the apple while Eve, with a knowing smile on her face, strikes a seductive pose, leaning slightly backwards with one arm holding on to a branch of the tree. The serpent looks directly at Eve, making it quite clear who is the evil party.

In some illustrations, the snake even takes the shape of a woman. Satan was usually depicted as a male reptile, but as early as the eighth century some painted boards, murals and book illuminations portrayed Eve's tempter as a serpent with the face and bust of a woman.[2] A female snake winds around the apple tree in the allegorical print *Adam and Eve in America* (1590), a depiction of sin in the innocent 'new found land of Virginia'.[3] In the central panel of his *Triptych of the Judgement* (1504), the Netherlandish artist Hieronymus Bosch depicts the serpent as a full-bodied woman with breasts and a long reptilian tail, handing the apple to Adam and Eve. The term 'Adam's apple' suggests that the bulge in a man's throat came from a piece of that fateful apple, and since it begins to protrude in puberty, it alludes to the old story that a woman was originally responsible for arousing male sexuality.

Women and apples also have a bad association in Greek mythology. As in the Garden of Eden, the myth of Atalanta is another story of apples leading a woman to an unhappy end. The beautiful maiden Atalanta vowed never to marry, but, at her father's request, agreed that

An 1810s book illustration of Atalanta and Hippomenes. Atalanta, bending to pick up a golden apple, loses the race to Hippomenes.

A scene from the Judgement of Paris is depicted in this tin-glazed, French, late 16th-century earthenware plate. Paris is shown presenting the golden apple to Aphrodite, the act that initiated the Trojan War.

she would marry any man who could outrun her in a race. One of her suitors, Hippomenes, prayed for help from Aphrodite, goddess of love and marriage, who gave him three golden apples and told him to drop them one at a time during the race to distract Atalanta. The trick worked; Hippomenes won the race and afterwards made love to Atalanta. But the petulant Aphrodite then turned them both into lions.

The Judgement of Paris is another mythological tale of an apple turned bad in the hands of women. Eris, the goddess of discord, started the Trojan War by tossing a golden apple inscribed 'to the fairest' on to the table at a banquet held by Zeus, king of the gods. Three beautiful guests, the goddesses Hera, Athena and Aphrodite, each claimed the apple. Zeus appointed Paris of Troy to decide which one deserved the title. They each posed nude before him, tempting him with both beauty and bribes. But he chose Aphrodite because she offered him Helen of Sparta, the most beautiful woman in the world, as his wife. His decision led to the war between Troy and Sparta and made the apple a lasting symbol of strife and sexual desire. The myth was an appealing subject for major artists from the Middle Ages to the twentieth century, including Rubens, Renoir, Watteau and Dalí. The pious Cranach the Elder painted more than two dozen versions of the shapely nudes; at the time (during the fifteenth century) the story was considered to be an allegory of marriage and the importance of choosing virtue over pleasure, an interpretation that is hard to agree with today.[4]

For both women and men in mythology, folklore and the arts, the apple has been a tempting representation of the desire for everything from power to carnal pleasure. As Thoreau summarizes, 'goddesses are fabled to have contended for it, dragons were set to watch it, and heroes were employed to pluck it.'[5] To Thoreau and Emily Dickinson (1830–1886), both writers of the New England apple landscape, the fruit forever out of Tantalus' reach was an apple. 'According to Homer,' Thoreau says, 'apples were among the fruits which Tantalus could not pluck, the wind ever blowing their boughs away from him.'[6] Dickinson alludes to the myth of Tantalus in the first stanza of her poem 'Heaven is What I Cannot Reach!':

> The Apple on the Tree–
> Provided it do hopeless – hang–
> That – 'Heaven' is – to Me!

Other poets have made the apple more graphically sexual, including Aristophanes, one of many classical writers who compared women's breasts to apples. But as portrayed by Bosch in his triptych depicting man's descent into hell, *The Garden of Earthly Delights* (*c.* 1500–1505), apples are fruits of carnal indulgence. In the central panel of this bizarre panorama, apples are among the giant fruits and other foods devoured and strangely inhabited by hordes of tiny nude figures.[7] In John Milton's masterpiece *Paradise Lost* (1667), Satan, disguised as the serpent, lures Eve to the apple by describing his own desire for the fruit as a sensual, irresistible hunger:

> To satisfy the sharp desire I had
> Of tasting those fair apples, I resolved
> Not to defer; hunger and thirst at once,
> Powerful persuaders, quickened at the scent
> Of that alluring fruit, urged me so keen.
> (Book IX, lines 584–8)

Once Eve gives in to this persuasive speech, Milton describes her eating of the apple as an act of gluttony: 'Greedily she ingorged without restraint' (line 791).

Even the genre paintings of boys in apple trees throwing the fruit down to girls may not be as innocent as they appear. According to some folk traditions, tossing an apple into a woman's lap was an invitation to sex. Cézanne's famous apples might also have had erotic implications for the artist. In his essay 'The Apples of Cézanne' (1968), Meyer Schapiro points out that apples had become erotic representations for the artist as a young man, in his reading of classical love poetry and in his amorous letters to both men and women. Focusing on the painting *The Amorous Shepherd* (1883–5), in which a young man hands an armful of apples to a nude woman, one of four sensual females surrounding him, Schapiro raises the following question:

> The central place given to the apples in a theme of love invites a question about the emotional ground of his frequent painting of apples. Does not the association here of

fruit and nudity permit us to interpret Cézanne's habitual choice of still-life – which means, of course, the apples – as a displaced erotic interest?[8]

Schapiro sees apples as a sexual symbol throughout Western culture:

> One can entertain more readily the idea of links between the painting of apples and sexual fantasy since in Western folklore, poetry, myth, language and religion, the apple has a familiar erotic sense . . . Through its attractive body, beautiful in color, texture and form, by its appeal to all the senses and promise of physical pleasure, the fruit is a natural analogue of ripe human beauty.[9]

Cézanne's contemporary Paul Gauguin gleefully surrounded himself with the trappings of both virtue and original sin in a strange self-portrait of 1889, painted on a cupboard door at an inn where he was staying in France. A halo hovers over his disembodied head, while a hand holds a snake and apples float in the background.

Lost Innocence

Gauguin's self-portrait is yet another artistic allusion to the Garden of Eden, but that iconic story is not always about sin. To the archaeologist Juris Zarins, the story of lost innocence in the Garden of Eden is something quite apart from sex. He believes it was a symbol of the revolutionary turning point in man's relationship with nature – the shift from hunter-gatherer to farmer. Eden was a place where man could freely collect and enjoy the fruits of nature. Once cast out, he had to feed himself by his own labour of growing crops. Told from the point of view of the hunter-gatherers, according to Zarins's theory, the tale passed into collective memory and found expression in the Bible.[10] It re-emerged in many other forms, including the Romantic movement's view of Native Americans as noble savages in the Eden

Paul Gauguin, *Self portrait*, 1889, oil on wood. The artist is surrounded
with the trappings of both virtue, a halo, and original sin: a snake and apples.

of the New World. In view of American history, Native Americans can easily be seen as Adam and Eve displaced from their Eden by white settlers planting apple orchards on tribal hunting grounds.

Yet the moral message of the Garden of Eden remained pervasive even as fundamentalist interpretation gave way in the nineteenth and twentieth centuries to more progressive thinking. While Bronson Alcott's ideas about raising children were fairly liberal for his nineteenth-century era, he firmly believed in teaching self-control to his children. In an apple anecdote from Louisa May Alcott's life, the biographer James Matteson notes that Bronson presented his young daughters with a morality lesson by acting out a child's version of the Fall of mankind. He placed an apple before them and, before leaving the room, told them that it was forbidden. On two occasions the three-year-old Louisa ate it, saying 'Me must have it.'[11]

The origin of the 'Big Apple', the nickname for New York City, was also infected by the Garden of Eden myth. Conventional wisdom has it that the name began in a city bordello in which the madam and prostitutes were known as 'Eve and her apples'. However, the source was another vice: horse racing. A sports writer in New York popularized the term in the 1920s as the top prize money for the city's races, 'the dream of every lad that ever threw a leg over a thoroughbred and the goal of all horsemen'.[12] From the racetracks it spread to Broadway theatre, ragtime and jazz, and in the 1970s to the New York Convention and Visitors Bureau, which made it successful in the promotion of tourism. However, during the city's fiscal crisis of that same decade, a cartoon depicted an apple eaten to the core. In the 1990s the Garden of Eden symbolism surfaced once again in the city's campaign against AIDS, with prevention posters displaying a serpent wrapped around an apple.

Happily, things are looking up a little for Eve. A drawing of 2008, one of several depicting a more modern view of the story, shows a woman in contemporary dress under an apple tree, with a firm grasp on a leashed serpent. In 2012 widespread media coverage of a sex scandal in the USA once again evoked the image of Eve as a temptress

Eve appears as a modern woman in this contemporary drawing.

leading a man to his fall. The man, David Petraeus, head of the U.S. Central Intelligence Agency and a retired four-star general, had resigned his CIA post after admitting to an extramarital affair with his biographer, Paula Broadwell. A number of reporters maintained that Broadwell, like Eve, should not have been 'so pushy with the apple'. However, the *New York Times* columnist Frank Bruni, using the slogan for a popular vegetable juice, observed: 'But then Adam could have had a V-8.'[13]

Egregious Grafts

Like the sinful apple itself, the method of growing apple trees from a graft has also come under attack at different times. Thoreau thought it was unnatural, but hundreds of years before he expressed his objections, the idea of combining two different plants had provoked a sense of deeper unease or even revulsion. Many saw it as an ungodly act, based on a prohibition in the Old Testament: 'You shall not sow your field with two kinds of seed, nor wear a garment upon you of two kinds of material mixed together' (Leviticus 19:19). In 1536 the French botanist Jean Ruel described grafting as 'adulterous insertions' – an odd reaction to asexual propagation.[14]

Nearly two centuries later, in 1716, the English gardener Thomas Fairchild created the first man-made hybrid by placing pollen from a sweet william on to the stigma of a carnation. The seed ripened inside the carnation and ultimately produced a flower with the characteristics of both plants. It was an amazing achievement in scientific observation and experimentation at a time when most gardeners were still following the flawed advice of ancient horticultural treatises. Many apple growers of Fairchild's day believed, for example, that apples could be made sweeter by urinating on the tree. (They may have been on to something, admittedly, since urea spray is used today on apple trees as a nitrogen fertilizer and to prevent disease.) Although Fairchild simply performed the role of the bee, he feared that he had violated God's laws of nature, and instead of rejoicing about his creation he worried that he had contradicted the universally held belief that only God could create new species. He 'lived in fear of God's wrath for the rest of his life'.[15] By the end of the century, another British botanist, Thomas Andrew Knight, was more sophisticated about his apple hybridization programme. In 1790 Knight and his daughter Frances conducted the first controlled cross-fertilizations, patiently crossing different apple varieties and clearly identifying the parents of the new generation. Discomfort with mixing plants has resurfaced in today's debate about genetically modified organisms, including the breeding of apples by transferring genes from one plant to another.

Black Magic

Frank Browning speaks of 'magic beneath the gold and crimson skin of that insufferably wholesome apple', and in folklore and fairy tales, it is often a case of black magic.[16] In the Grimms' fairy tale of Snow White (1812), evil lurks once again within an apple, poisoned by a wicked queen who, like the vain goddesses of the Judgement of Paris, will do anything to claim the title of 'fairest of all'. While the queen poses as a farmer's wife in the Grimm tale, the Disney film of 1937 portrays her as a witch who brews a magic cocktail that temporarily transforms her into a hunchbacked crone. Holding out the poisoned fruit to Snow White, she cackles, 'This is no ordinary apple. It's a magic wishing apple. One bite and all your dreams will come true.' The apple was both red and green, but the queen had poisoned the red side to make it more appealing. One bite from that deceptive side sent Snow White into a nightmare of death-like sleep. The concept of the poisoned apple may arise from the fact that the fruit's seeds contain a little cyanide, the cause of their bitter taste. Browning speculates that it became a theme in folklore after the fall of Rome, when bitter apples became 'just the sort of thing a witch would feed to an innocent girl'.[17] Long before then, warnings against eating wild apples had appeared in ancient Greek and Roman texts from Hippocrates' *Regimen* (400 BC) to Pliny's *Natural History* (AD 77–9).[18] Although cultivated sweet apples were widely enjoyed during Pliny's time, in his list of the varieties growing in Italy, he warned of one with a 'horrible sourness . . . so powerful that it will blunt the edge of a sword'.[19] Sour or unripe apples are often green, a fact that led Snow White to choose the red half of the poisoned apple. Generations of parents have told their children that eating green apples leads to stomach ache. Although unripe green apples with their high levels of acid can cause gastric distress, the fear of green apples seems to

Snow White bomber. As shown in this 1943 photo, the story of Snow White and
the poisoned apple took an even more lethal form in the Second World War bomber
christened with her name and image. The plane, photographed here at the U.S. Air
Force Base in the Libyan desert, flew 36 bombing missions over the Middle East.

have disappeared with the popularity of the Granny Smith. This
Australian cultivar is so well known today that it has become a distinctive flavour in an alcoholic drink not usually associated with
apples. The makers of Van Gogh Vodka describe their product as
'infused with fresh ripe green apples from the Netherlands . . . with
a taste similar to Granny Smith apples'.[20]

Bad Apple Redux

Whether green or red, the apple that poisoned Snow White has
become an apt symbol of the fear of chemical contamination in apple
agriculture today. Critics such as the writer Roger Yepsen claim that
'growers have sprayed the daylights out of a few marketable varieties',
in a process that continues through every stage of growth and storage:

Spraying apple orchards, New Jersey, 1935, stereoscopic card. The average apple is sprayed with chemicals more than a dozen times in a single growing season.

'The average apple is sprayed twelve times on the tree and embalmed under wax or shellac', he complains.[21] Chemical sprays are used not only to kill insects and prevent disease, but also to induce trees to shed small apples and produce larger ones, and – in a process alarmingly called bin drenching – to prevent the harvest from rotting during storage.

Apple pesticides are not new; as early as the Enlightenment, Browning explains, 'gardeners were painting their fruit trees with a variety of poisonous unctions dedicated to the death of insects.'[22] By the 1880s French horticulturists had developed recipes for two effective and widely used sprays: Bordeaux Mixture or hydrated copper sulphate, used to treat mould on grapes and apples; and Paris Green or ferrous sulphate, a toxic emerald-green powder once used to kill rats in Paris sewers (and also as a pigment by Impressionist painters), used for apples as an insecticide.[23] In the U.S., apple growers soon adopted both, and blended Paris Green with lead arsenate to control the codling moth. It took a century for the U.S. to ban arsenic and lead sprays on food, in the 1980s, but such substances pose a continuing threat. These heavy metals do not degrade, and remain in the soil (and the human body) virtually indefinitely. They pose a lingering problem in old orchards and have raised new alarms about the massive amount of apple juice imported from China, where it is suspected by scientists that growers might still be using the arsenate sprays. Tests conducted in the U.S. in 2009–10 on imported Chinese juice discovered high levels of arsenic in a number of samples, and the continuing flow of juice from China remains a serious concern.[24]

Browning recalls seeing apple trees being sprayed with lime sulphur in his family orchards in Kentucky in the 1950s:

> A high yellow plume would shoot up above the apple trees,
> a Day-Glo mist against the dark band of forest that lurked
> beneath the sky. Lime sulfur was what we used then, and
> pretty as it was, it stank like a ton of rotten egg yolks.[25]

Sulphur was used to smother tiny insect eggs and fungal spores before they awakened each spring, and was just the first of a series of sprays that continued throughout the growing season in the never-ending battle against destructive bugs and disease. Today it has been replaced by many different chemical pesticides and fungicides, some colourless and odourless. But sulphur and copper, both noxious to humans in large doses, are still in use, surprisingly even in some organic apple orchards in the U.S., where government standards consider them acceptable 'natural' preventions.

The Snow White theme of the poisoned apple has reappeared in both real life and film. In 1954 the English mathematician Alan Turing, one of the inventors of the digital computer and a key figure in breaking the Nazis' codes during the Second World War, died of self-inflicted cyanide poisoning. A half-eaten apple was found beside his bed, and, although it was not tested for the poison, it was suspected to have been the means of the fatal dose. According to his friend the novelist Alan Garner, Turing was fascinated with the Disney film of the Snow White story, especially the transformation of the wicked queen into the witch and the ambiguity of the poisoned apple, red on one side and green on the other.[26] The film *Snow White and the Huntsman* (2012), a radically different treatment from that of the animated Disney version, takes place in a dystopian landscape of environmental degradation – a suitable place for an apple poisoned by chemicals. The new Snow White has undergone a transformation, too, but a much happier one. No longer a powerless victim, she has become a warrior, tough enough to overcome the wicked queen and the poisoned apple.

Bad Company

Apples have also been tainted by association in a number of twentieth-century advertisements for unhealthy and even toxic products. In the 1940s a series of illustrated magazine ads combined apples with Old Gold cigarettes. The first featured drawings of cut apples dripping tiny drops of juice on to the cigarette packages, and, while entreating readers to 'Buy more war bonds now', the text boasted: 'Apple honey now protects Old Gold freshness.' In another ad, an American sailor and his girlfriend are riding in a horse-drawn carriage under a bough of apple blossom. The message there is 'The flowers that bloom in the spring bring apple honey to Old Golds.' Another featuring a similar couple strikes a romantic note: 'Apple honey and freshness go together like moonlight and roses!' Today the ads seem oxymoronic, but during the war years they were a clever way to take advantage of the shortage of glycerine, used as a moistening agent in tobacco. The ads made the substitution clear – and took pride in the change. The term 'apple honey' was also a cunning suggestion of soothing a smoker's cough:

> This new moistening agent is a mellow, golden, honey-like syrup – from fresh, pure apple juice. It's so much like honey, we named it Apple 'Honey'. Sprayed on our choice Old Gold tobacco, Apple 'Honey' penetrates every fragrant, flavorful shred, helps keep them moist, pliable and FRESH on their way to you. Apple 'Honey' is tasteless. Therefore it does not change the taste of Old Golds. In many ways, we think it superior to glycerin.

Another *NEW*[*] has been Added!

Apple "Honey" Now Protects Old Gold Freshness

NO CHANGE IN TASTE!

Old Gold CIGARETTES

THE TREASURE OF THEM ALL

P. Lorillard Company— Established 1760

BUY MORE WAR BONDS NOW!

LOWEST IN NICOTINE
LOWEST IN THROAT-IRRITATING TARS AND RESINS

As shown by unbiased, independent, unsolicited tests of 7 leading brands —made for Reader's Digest.

APPLE "HONEY" is our name for an amazing new moistening agent which helps hold in the freshness of Old Gold cigarettes.

It has been developed by evaporating the pure, golden juice of fresh, luscious apples to a bland, honey-like syrup. Lightly sprayed on tobacco, this extract penetrates every particle to help hold in the moisture after the cigarette is made.

We call this latest Old Gold triumph *Apple "Honey."* We're using *Apple "Honey"* now to protect Old Gold freshness. All in all, we believe it superior to glycerine, which is now needed at the battlefront.

Apple "Honey". is not a flavoring . . . does not change the taste of Old Golds. You enjoy the same delicious flavor — the same fine tobaccos, including Latakia. *Apple "Honey"* simply helps to keep Old Golds fresh on their way to you.

> [*]New moisture-protecting agent developed by U. S. Department of Agriculture. We call it Apple "Honey."

SAME FINE TOBACCOS—INCLUDING LATAKIA

'Apple Honey' cigarettes, poster, c. 1940s. Advertisers took full advantage of the wartime shortage of glycerin, the traditional moisturizing agent for tobacco, by substituting apple juice.

Children from the UN Nursery School receive apples, 1949.
Note that the man handing out apples is also holding a cigarette.

In another disingenuous advertisement, the Shell Chemical Corporation promoted its fertilizers with the slogan 'Picks up where Johnny Appleseed left off.' The ad, which appeared in 1959, carried a drawing of Appleseed holding a giant apple, and claimed that he 'never saw fruit so fine'. The 'secret of today's wonder crop', the text explains, is Shell Chemical's 'nitrogen-rich fertilizers'. And, it goes on to say, modern orchardists relying on the fertilizers were not the only ones following in Appleseed's footsteps. Like the legendary hero, Shell Chemical was a pioneer. 'Next time you bite into a juicy, crackling apple, remember that modern Johnny Appleseeds can always count on their partner Shell Chemical – pioneer in ammonia fertilizers.'

The apple's reputation might have suffered rather from keeping company with cigarettes and fertilizers, but it truly went downhill in a cereal campaign that portrayed the apple itself as the villain. In 2006 the Kellogg Company began television and internet cartoon ads trying to convince children that Apple Jacks tasted more like cinnamon than like apples. A cinnamon-stick figure called 'CinnaMon', a slim, cool character who spoke with a West Indian accent and rode on a skateboard, raced a squat, grouchy 'Bad Apple' towards a bowl of the cereal. The sour-faced, scheming apple threw obstacles in CinnaMon's path, but always failed to beat him. At the end of the ad, CinnaMon explained: 'Apple Jacks don't taste like apples because the sweet taste of cinnamon is the winner, mon.' The ads drew complaints and the threat of a lawsuit from the Children's Advertising Review Unit (CARU), a U.S. foundation that monitors ads and also supports a five-a-day fruit campaign. CARU officials complained that Kellogg put apples on the package to attract parents, but at the same time went behind the parents' backs to tell children, 'Don't worry. They don't taste like apples.'[27] The company denied CARU's charges but eventually agreed to change the ads, making the apple character 'frustrated rather than mean-spirited' and adding that they would no longer call him 'bad'. Kellogg appeared to be trapped between the belief that children do not like the idea of a fruit cereal and unwillingness to give up the well-known apple name. For a time the two cartoon characters were competitive friends, reaching the bowl of Apple Jacks at the same time. But in 2013 Kellogg introduced another type of cereal, Cinnamon Jacks, with CinnaMon as its sole mascot. Apple Jacks, which are made with a little dried apple and apple juice concentrate – less than the amount of salt they contain – are still sold with a happier-looking apple cartoon on the box; yet even without cinnamon, the cereal tastes more like sugar – its largest ingredient (43 per cent of the cereal) – than apples.[28]

Helge Lundstrom, portrait of Linnaeus composed of 2,000 apples, Sweden, 1998.
Ironically, Linnaeus believed that the fruit in the Garden of Eden was a banana.

nine

Misplaced Apples

When we talk about a false analogy, a comparison of incomparables, we say: 'It's like comparing apples and oranges.' But in a number of curious cases, the same could be said of comparing apples and apples. Since biblical times many of the fruits called apples have possibly or actually been something quite different from what they seem. These so-called apples could be figs, pomegranates, quinces, pears, bananas or even – to go beyond fruit – a cracker, a record label or a computer.

Although the Book of Genesis does not specify what fruit grew on the Tree of Knowledge in the Garden of Eden, the ancient Hebrew word *tappuah*, which appears in several other books of the Old Testament, has been translated as 'apple'. In the first five books of the Old Testament, known as the Torah, the word is generally explained as the place of an apple tree, as in the ancient city of Ephraim, once part of Palestine. But a number of scholars have pointed out that *tappuah* meant a place where a different fruit grew, more likely a fig, quince or grape.[1] The eighteenth-century botanist Carl Linnaeus, the founder of botanical taxonomy, came up with the most original alternative to the biblical apple: a banana. All these fruits seem more likely to have grown in the hot climate of the Levant.

Some historians, assuming the Garden had a geographically specific location, have come up with intriguing theories on the identity of the apple – most of them tropical rather than cold-weather fruit. The Bible is fairly specific about the location of the garden near four rivers, including two that still run today, the Euphrates and the Hiddekel, now known as the Tigris (Genesis 2:10–14). Some theories place it in modern-day Iraq or Iran (where the two rivers run today) or where they rise in the mountains of Turkey, a more hospitable climate for apples than Palestine. (Mormons, all on their own in these theories, believe it was near today's city of St Louis, Missouri.) Juris Zarins, the archaeologist who saw the Garden of Eden as a parable of the change from foraging to farming, employed scientific methods to map the location of the garden. Using satellite imagery to track the vestiges of the waterways, he pinpointed Saudi Arabia, in a once-fertile valley overtaken thousands of years ago by the Persian Gulf.[2] Fertile or not, this hot southern location would seem to be an unlikely birthplace for the cold-craving apple – and a more plausible home, according to Linnaeus's theory, for the banana. Some varieties of apple, such as Winter Banana, are named for their banana flavour. (There are apple-flavoured bananas, as well.) But Linnaeus scoffed at the idea of any apple in the Garden of Eden. He believed in Eden and he believed the fruit that grew there was a banana. Not surprisingly, Dan Koeppel, the popular science writer who wrote a book about the banana, embraces the botanist's theory with great enthusiasm. He believes that the Latin names Linnaeus gave to two different varieties of banana provide telling clues to the Garden of Eden. Linnaeus called the common yellow banana *Musa sapientum*, meaning 'banana of knowledge', which Koeppel sees as a reference to the Tree of Knowledge, and the green banana or plantain *Musa paradisiaca*, 'banana of paradise'.[3] Koeppel argues that 'the banana is lush, tropical, and sexually suggestive, more tempting, in a purely allegorical sense, than the apple.'[4] And for anyone who is still not convinced, he adds a practical argument. The fig leaves that Adam and Eve supposedly used to cover their nakedness would barely cover the essentials. Big banana leaves would have been much more effective.

Doubts have also been raised about the apple of classical Greek mythology. In one of the most famous passages in the *Odyssey*, Homer describes Odysseus' refuge in King Alcinous' garden of fruit trees

RESPICE·FINEM

Heinrich Aldegrever, *Respice Finem* (Look to the End), engraving, c. 1530.
The nude in this memento mori (reminder of death) recalls Eve's sin as a symbol
of mortality, but the figure holds a pomegranate rather than an apple.

where, depending on the translation, the apple trees bear 'a glossy burden' or 'the reddening apples ripen to gold.' Written in the eighth or ninth century BC, the passage is often cited as the first literary mention of the apple in the ancient world. But the linguist and historian Andrew Dalby points out that the Greek word *melon*, which is commonly translated as 'apple', could just as well have signified quince, lemon or any other round fruit grown at the time.[5] The theory would take the apple out of Alcinous' orchard and the garden of the Hesperides, and would place an unknown round fruit in Paris' hand as he extends it to Aphrodite, and in Atalanta's path as she pauses in her race with Hippomenes.

All this fruit confusion, many scholars have speculated, could have started with some literal-minded monks translating Latin texts. As the Old Testament made its way from ancient Hebrew to Greek, Latin and medieval English translations, the monks may have associated the Latin word for apple, *malum*, with the Latin *malus*, meaning evil, typecasting the apple forever after as the embodiment of sin. Once the image took graphic form in paintings by Renaissance artists, it was imprinted in our understanding of the Bible, Greek myths and many different expressions of popular folklore. Picturing a different fruit in the Garden of Eden could restore the apple's good name, but it is now hard to imagine a fig, quince, lemon, grape or banana hanging from the Tree of Knowledge, shot by William Tell's arrow, eaten by Snow White or falling on Newton's head.

Peter Stuyvesant's 'Apple Tree'

One of the oldest apple trees in America, so the story goes, was planted in the mid-seventeenth century in modern-day New York City by Peter Stuyvesant (1612–1672), the director-general of the Dutch colony of New Netherlands from 1647 to 1664, the year the British took over and renamed it New York. The story of this apple tree and its long life appears in virtually the same form in many books and on websites about apple history, horticulture and culinary arts, but it is apparently a case of mistaken identity. The oft-repeated story goes like this: Stuyvesant, a famous figure in the early history of the city, brought the tree from his native Holland and planted it on his farm in either 1647 or 1667, according to different versions of the tale (the latter is the year the British allowed the former governor to return to his farm, where he lived peacefully for the rest of his days). The tree outlasted Stuyvesant by two centuries; in 1862, *Harper's Monthly Magazine* called it 'the oldest living thing in the City of New York'.[6] It stood its ground for more than 200 years amid new buildings and increasing traffic, as the area became the busy commercial corner of Third Avenue and Thirteenth Street in Manhattan. But it came to a violent end in 1867 when it was forcefully hit by a horse-drawn wagon, and uprooted.

The tree is no longer there to prove the story and, if it were, it would reveal a slightly different tale – and a different fruit. According to a bronze plaque first mounted at the site in 1890, the tree bore fruit right up to its demise, but pears, not apples. In fact, the plaque was mounted in a pharmacy on the site, known as the Pear Tree Drugstore. In 2003 New York City officials planted an actual pear tree on the site, designating it as 'Pear Tree Corner'. Nonetheless, the story of Stuyvesant's apple tree lives on in many publications, despite the fact that a slice of the original pear tree's trunk, enclosed in a glass case, has been in the collections of the New-York Historical Society for years, donated by a descendant of Stuyvesant. But advocates of the apple tree theory may take hope. The image of the pear relic in the society's digital archives includes a caveat: 'Due to ongoing research, information about this object is subject to change.'[7]

In Name Only

The apple was so well known that its name was given to a number of other fruits, even those completely different in taste and appearance – and some that are highly toxic. Tomatoes and potatoes were given apple-related names after the sixteenth-century Spanish conquistadores

Thorn apple, watercolour, Rome, c. 1622–3. One of many 'apples' in name only.

brought them from Central and South America to Europe. The first tomatoes to arrive were small and yellow and were called 'apples of gold', *pome d'oro*. Italians readily adopted tomatoes and still call them *pomodoro*. While the French know them as *tomates*, they still call the potato *pomme de terre*, apple of the earth. The English were slow to accept the tomato, with its astringent taste and strong smell, as an edible fruit. John Gerard called them 'apples of love' and said they were a dangerous, possibly poisonous aphrodisiac that offered 'very little nourishment to the body, and the same naught and corrupt'.[8] He also had little use for plants that he called 'madde apples', perhaps related to today's aubergine, and 'thornie apples', a weed-like plant with a small fruit:

I rather wish English men to content themselves with the meat and sauce of our owne country, than with fruit and sauce eaten with such peril; for doubtlesse these Apples have mischievous qualities, the use whereof is utterly to bee forsaken.[9]

Gerard would be amazed to learn that his 'apples of love', although not commonly considered a fruit, are today the world's largest fruit crop. In 2010 some 141 million tons of tomatoes were produced, most of them made into sauce or paste, compared to 69 million tons of apples.

Also viewed with great suspicion was the apple of Sodom, as its name implies. Medieval pilgrims returning from Palestine said they had seen it growing near the Dead Sea at what they believed to be the sites of the ancient cities of Sodom and Gomorrah.[10] The association with these wicked places proved to be a useful warning. Although it is in the same family as the tomato and aubergine, the apple of Sodom (*Solanum sodomeum*; now *S. linnaeanum*) is a species of nightshade and yields poisonous fruit. The May apple (*Podophyllum peltatum*), a herbaceous plant that pops up like a little umbrella in the forests of northeast America, bears round, yellow fruits that are also deadly if eaten. Like actual apples, the sorb apple, a small, edible red fruit, grows on a tree (*Sorbus domestica*). It is also known as the service tree or Juneberry. Two other 'apples' of South America, the wolf apple of Brazil and the pineapple, are highly palatable. The pineapple, a prized fruit in Victorian greenhouses, apparently took its name from its pine-cone shape and juicy fruit. The wolf apple (*Solanum lycocarpum*) is in fact eaten by wolves in Brazil, and the human population also relishes it for fruit preserves. Recent studies have found it to be more nutritious than apples themselves.[11]

There are no apples in Ritz Crackers' Mock Apple Pie, but at least the name does not pretend to be something other than it is, a mock version of the dish. It was invented in the 1930s, soon after Ritz Crackers were introduced to the American market, and the recipe was on the back of the box for decades. Made mostly of crackers and sugar syrup, with a little cinnamon, it tasted surprisingly like apple pie, albeit not one of the best. It was created during the years of the Great Depression ostensibly as an economical dish, although apples, sold on many American street corners during that time, were hardly in short supply. Ritz probably just saw it as a good way to sell a lot of crackers.

René Magritte's *Son of Man* painting recreated with apples and other fruits and vegetables by Alon Zaid, 2011. Magritte's apple paintings turned the apple into a graphic icon that inspired The Beatles' Apple Records logo.

Two of the most powerful companies in the music and technological industries, The Beatles' Apple Corps and the computer giant Apple, Inc., fought for more than two decades to control the apple logo. It all began with the Surrealist artist René Magritte, whose portrayal of green apples transformed the fruit into a logo. Magritte's paintings of a uniformly green apple as a giant fruit filling an entire room (*The Listening Room*, 1952) and, most famously, obscuring a man's face in his so-called self portrait *The Son of Man* (1964), made the green apple an iconic graphic image. One of his lesser-known green-apple paintings, *The Game of Mora* (*Le Jeu de Morre*, 1966), was given to Paul McCartney as a gift in the 1960s and inspired The Beatles' Apple Corps logo and its pun on 'apple core'.[12] The Surrealist's departure from conventional art apparently appealed to The Beatles' sense of themselves as free spirits of the music industry.

The apple also appealed to Steve Jobs in the 1970s, when he was searching for a name for his new computer company – and it had an alphabetical advantage, placing Apple Computer, later Apple, Inc.,

Apple Computer logo, 2009. The bite out of the apple represents a computer byte.

'Keep Your Lawyers Off My Computer', a campaign button produced
by Apple Computers in the 1980s as part of their lawsuit against the
Beatles Apple Corps for trademark rights to the apple logo.

first in advertising listings. Apple's first product, the Macintosh
computer (1984), was named after the McIntosh apple, a favourite
of the computer's primary inventor, Jef Raskin, but the spelling was
changed for copyright reasons.[13] The company's first logo was a vin-
tage-looking drawing of Isaac Newton sitting under an apple tree,
presumably with the implication that great minds think alike. It evolved
over the years to a graphic apple in various colours, including a trendy
rainbow, and ultimately to the familiar apple with a bite out of it, a
pun on the computer byte.

Although the logos on the music labels and computers were not
the same design, they were similar enough for lawyers to create a
prolonged battle for the trademark of the image, more determined
and costly than any fight for market control of the actual fruit. The
fight turned nasty at times and inevitably drew on the image of the
serpent in the Garden of Eden. In the late 1980s and early '90s,
Apple, Inc., distributed a campaign badge depicting a snake with its
fangs bared coiled inside a rainbow-coloured apple, with the slogan
'Keep Your Lawyers Off My Computer.' The tug of war continued
for 23 years, outlasting two of The Beatles and finally ending in 2007

in a settlement that allowed Jobs's company to purchase The Beatles' apple logo and license it back to Apple Corps. The following year Jobs's company also challenged New York City's application for the trademark of the stylized green-apple emblem used for many years in the city's environmental programme, GreeNYC. Apple, Inc., settled when the city removed a leaf from its apple. In 2012, a year after Jobs's death, the official process was finally completed, making his company the registered owner of the apple logo for use in a wide range of products and services.

'If You're Screwy Vote for Dewey', campaign sticker for the re-election of
Franklin D. Roosevelt as U.S. President in 1936. It linked the apple, a powerful
symbol of the Depression, with FDR's opponent, Thomas Dewey.

ten

The Politics of Pomology

The apple has been a pawn in the politics of the past two centuries, from nineteenth-century American patriotism to the poverty of the Great Depression and the policies of multinational corporations. At times it has been pummelled by the two greatest political forces of the twentieth century, American capitalism and Soviet communism. Although at odds with each other in every way, these ideologies unwittingly combined almost to wipe out the apple's best qualities.

Apples planted on the American frontier were a patriotic symbol of the country's expansionist fervour. To many nineteenth-century Americans, moving into the frontier and, in the process, moving Native Americans out was the nation's 'Manifest Destiny', a policy sanctioned by the religious, racial and political ideals of the day. More than half a century after Johnny Appleseed's westward excursions, the author of a sentimental biography about Chapman, *The Romance of the Sower* (1915), still portrayed the displacement of Native Americans as an 'honorable' part of American empire building:

> His day was that of the pioneers who crossed the Alleghany Mountains; of the river boatmen who navigated the uncharted waterways of the old Northwest Territory, and of the Indian-fighters of the last border wars. All of these played their honorable parts in the winning of an empire of forest and prairie.[1]

Not long after the Native Americans were pushed out, however, the forces of industrialization began to exert pressure on small farmers. As canals, railways and refrigeration technology swept across the country, the apple was no longer just one of many diverse crops grown on small farms. It was a national commodity, supported both by big business interests and by government officials who believed in a new set of agricultural goals. As early as the first decades of the nineteenth century, agricultural reformers were urging farmers to think of apples as commodities, advising them through articles in a spate of new horticultural journals to swap their seedlings for more profitable orchards of grafted trees.[2] And once they did, attitudes to the sharing of apples also changed in the culture generally and in the legal system. Picking apples off someone else's trees, called scrumping in England, was a crime there in the nineteenth century and could lead to penalties as severe as deportation to Australia.[3] But it was generally accepted in the U.S. as an innocent boyhood practice. Asking permission first was advised, but if boys neglected to do so, the penalties, if any, were trivial. Once farmers valued apples as a commercial crop, however, they began to lobby for laws to criminalize pilfering. In 1846 in the state of Ohio, where Johnny Appleseed had sold apple seedlings for pennies and on many occasions had given them away, a law was passed establishing fines and up to 60 days' imprisonment for those who damaged apple trees or stole the fruit.[4]

Apple Suckers

American families that could not afford expensive grafted trees when they moved westward planted seeds or seedlings, but the true sign of a poor farmer was the one who planted apple-tree suckers, the sprouts that shoot up from the base of the trunk. Orchardists see these as a nuisance, competing with the grown tree for food and water, and cut them down. But if a farmer setting out for the frontier had an apple tree back home, he would simply dig up a sucker and take it with him. Closely associated with the transient

A man sells apples near the U.S. Capitol in Washington, DC, 1930.
An apple industry group sold apples at a discount to the unemployed
so that they could earn some income during the Depression.

rural poor, the term 'sucker' soon took on a negative connotation
that continues today.[5]

During the Great Depression, apples also became a sign of poverty
as men who lost their jobs were forced to sell them on the street.
The image of a well-dressed, unemployed businessman hawking

apples for a nickel on a New York City street corner became an emotive symbol of difficult times for people at all economic levels. But, like much greater numbers of people caught in the Depression, the businessman selling apples turned out to be a sucker, a vulnerable figure manipulated by economic forces out of his control. As Daniel Okrent explains in his book *Great Fortune*, 'the International Apple Shippers' Association figured out how to dump its surplus by selling it on credit to the unemployed.'[6] The association donated $10,000 for the programme, which was conceived in New York during National Apple Week in 1930. The apples were sold to the unemployed at about 10 per cent below market cost. Initially, some of the unemployed vendors made money selling apples for as much as 50 cents each, but as the number of vendors increased to 5,000, the price dropped to a nickel. Their profit dropped further, James McWilliams explains in his essay 'Depression Apples', because they had to hire a cart or cab to transport the apples from the central pickup point in Manhattan to their street corners. The typical vendor made only about a penny an apple, but without other job opportunities, many kept going. By 1931 the association had run out of New York apples and had to buy more from Washington State, at higher prices. Many vendors then switched to shining shoes, a less dignified but slightly more profitable alternative. By the height of the Depression, the apple-selling craze was all but over, yet unemployed men selling apples, not shining shoes, remains the most striking image of those hard times. 'So why is it the apple peddler that gets all the glory?', McWilliams asks:

> I think the answer has to do with symbolism. There's something more noble in the image of two Americans standing together and exchanging a nickel for an apple than there is in one man hunched around the feet of another, face down, grunting it out.[7]

At its height, the Depression caused ten million Americans to lose their jobs. Yet the relatively few apple sellers on the streets of

America's largest city made the apple a powerful symbol of un-employment. In the presidential election of 1936, Franklin Delano Roosevelt's campaign cleverly associated it with his rival, Thomas Dewey. FDR's posters portrayed a large apple with the slogan 'If you're screwy, vote for Dewey.'

Campaign Apples

FDR's campaign was neither the first nor the last to make the apple a symbol in an American presidential election. In the mid-nineteenth century, while industrialization and capitalism were changing the American landscape, apples became a nostalgic sign of a simpler life – and a useful political tool. In 1840 the country was also in the throes of a depression, and the Whig candidate William Henry Harrison was running against the incumbent Democratic president, Martin Van Buren. Although Harrison lived on a grand estate in Virginia, surrounded by well-tended grafted apple orchards, his party portrayed him as the 'log cabin and hard cider' candidate who had the best interests of small farmers at heart. The claim was doubly ironic since the slogan was put forth in the midst of the Temperance Movement, which was forcing self-provisioning farmers to give up producing cider.[8] Nonetheless, nostalgia for a lost way of life apparently motivated voters looking for a simple way out of the depression, and they elected Harrison. In the election of 1952, after two decades of Democratic presidents, a cartoon depicted the Republican Party as the sleeping Snow White. The Democratic president, Harry Truman, was the witch with the poisoned apple, and the Republican candidate, Dwight Eisenhower, was the prince on horseback galloping to Snow White's rescue.

The apple and its well-known stories were moulded to fit many other political issues, as seen in a variety of satirical illustrations from different eras. In an English print of 1798, a fat John Bull, his pockets bulging with golden apples, stands under a tree hung with rotten apples labelled 'treason', 'slavery' and other evils, while a serpent with

'The Tree of Liberty, with the Devil tempting John Bull', 1798, print.

the face of the contemporary Whig politician Charles James Fox
holds out a damaged apple marked 'reform'. The Garden of Eden
appears in a magazine cover of 1883 attacking the corrupt Tammany
Hall politics of New York City, and in a cartoon of 1907 depicting
President Theodore ('Teddy') Roosevelt's campaign to dissolve the
monopolies of corporate trusts. In 1897, at the height of America's
imperialist drives, the satirical magazine *Puck* portrayed Uncle Sam
wearing a farmer's hat and standing under an apple tree, ready to
catch the apples labelled Hawaii, Cuba, Canada and Central America

Udo Keppler, 'In the Republican Eden', *Puck*, 1907. In this Garden of Eden setting, the naked figure crouching on the right is President Theodore Roosevelt, who was trying to dissolve corporate trusts yet wanted to enact trade tariffs. The angel in the centre represents the trusts forbidding Roosevelt to partake of the apple tree labelled 'The Tariff'.

in the very large basket at his feet. A cartoon of 1987 used apples to skewer President Ronald Reagan for the Iran–Contra scandal, in which his administration, in violation of Congressional restrictions, sent arms to Iran in exchange for American hostages and to the Nicaraguan Contras, an anti-communist force. The cartoon depicts Reagan signing the arms agreement and shielding his eyes as he asks, 'So this is a proclamation for National Apple Pie Week?' In 1990, during the campaign for East Germany's first parliamentary elections following the fall of Berlin, a Christian Democratic Union poster shows an apple with two worms, one on the left and one on the right, with the caption 'I am rankled by the Left and the Right.'

Cold War politics in America also exploited the apple and the legend of Johnny Appleseed. In the first half of the twentieth century, writers including the socialist author Howard Fast had celebrated Appleseed as a gentle American hero planting a path of apple orchards

THE TEMPTATION.

Gilliam Bernhard, 'The Temptation', *Puck*, 1883. The serpent in this Garden of Eden cartoon is New York City's corrupt Tammany Hall tempting the county democracy with the apple of 'harmony'.

Louis Dalrymple, 'Patient waiters are no losers', *Puck*, 1897.

through the wilderness. But during the post-war campaign against 'godless communism', Appleseed's heroism was defined by Christianity and American individualism. In the Disney film *The Legend of Johnny Appleseed* (1948), he carries a Bible emblazoned with a gold cross, along with his bag of apple seeds. The film, according to the historian William Kerrigan, is

> a near perfect sermon on postwar American values. Faith in God and the ability of the individual to make a difference in history are the central themes. Johnny celebrates American freedom, singing, 'Here I am 'neath the blue blue sky, doing as I please', thanking God for that freedom.[9]

Big Deals

Along with all its symbolic mutations, the apple itself was transformed in the twentieth century into a corporate product, one that was supported by government policies. One heirloom grower sees it as a 'sort of conspiracy'. In his book *Not Far from the Tree* (2007), John Bunker, a collector and grower of old apple varieties in Maine, explains that in 1927 state agricultural agents in New England created the 'New England Seven', a list of varieties they judged worthy of commercial production, and discouraged farmers from planting any other types.[10] The number of apple varieties continued to decline after the Second World War, as small family farms became increasingly vulnerable to big competition. By the 1970s, the national preference for big operations focusing on a few commercial varieties was made crystal clear when Earl Butz, the U.S. Secretary of Agriculture under Presidents Richard Nixon and Gerald Ford, warned American farmers to 'get big or get out' and created federal policies that favoured big farms. Together, the largest growers in the U.S. have been successful in securing government subsidy and legislation to benefit their operations. Ironically, as Kerrigan points out, the apple industry acts like a multinational corporation, while advertising its roots in family farms.[11]

The 'get big or get out' advice to apple growers in the U.S. was a warning that serious global competition was on the horizon. In the 1980s and '90s, about 20 per cent of American orchards went bankrupt because of rising imports from other countries: Granny Smiths from Australia, Galas and Braeburns from New Zealand, Fujis from Japan and apple juice concentrate from China.[12] And the U.S. apple industry was not the only one to depend on political support to get big. In the late 1980s the Beijing government fuelled the beginnings of China's apple boom. At the time Chinese apples, which were small and tasteless, were non-starters on the world market. But China began to import Red and Golden Delicious apples, and developed new techniques to improve its local varieties. Since then the global market for apples has followed an increasingly combative cycle of trading patterns and policies, not only in China. Japanese apple growers have been especially hostile towards imported apples, although they have not objected to using varieties developed in other countries to create their own hybrids. In the 1930s Japanese breeders developed the Mutsu apple, since renamed the Crispin, from a cross of the Golden Delicious and the Japanese Indo apple. The Fuji also originated in Japan, as a cross of two American apples, the Red Delicious and Ralls Genet, an eighteenth-century heirloom from Virginia. Yet Japan kept its borders closed to apple imports from all countries until 1971, and for the next three decades imposed extraordinarily rigid and costly sanitary regulations that effectively kept the imports out.[13] The restrictions finally ended through a World Trade Organization proceeding in 2005.

During the eighteenth and nineteenth centuries, British and European explorers had brought many plants and flowers from the Far East to the West. Today Japanese apples and Chinese juice are once again bringing the horticulture of the Far East, albeit somewhat changed, back to the West. Ironically, while U.S. growers today are urging trade restrictions to staunch the flow of Chinese apples, the fact that commercially grown apples were largely introduced to China as Western cultivars means that many Chinese today think of the apple as a foreign fruit.[14]

Pesticide Politics

Hand in hand with the mass production of apples, which depends upon an arsenal of chemicals, are the politics of pesticides. Beginning in the 1880s, when new chemical treatments were introduced to American apple growers, the U.S. Department of Agriculture was an 'enthusiastic champion' of the sprays and actively promoted them to farmers.[15] A century later, the public was keenly aware of the dangers of chemical sprays, such as DDT, and government agencies found themselves in the middle of major battles between industry and environmental groups. The controversy erupted in the apple industry in the so-called Alar scare of 1989–90. It began with a report by an environmental organization revealing that the chemical daminozise, known as Alar, which had been sprayed on apple trees in the USA for more than two decades, had been found to be carcinogenic at very high doses in laboratory tests. It was used primarily on red varieties of apple, particularly those grown on dwarf rootstocks, which tended to drop their apples before they were fully red. Sprayed with Alar, the fruit turned uniformly red without fully ripening, preventing drop, improving the fruit's appearance and extending its shelf life. The report received national exposure on a popular television show, and set off a general alarm. The actress Meryl Streep, the mother of small children at the time, publicly condemned the carcinogenic risk to children. The general outcry led the U.S. Environmental Protection Agency to ban the use of Alar – and apple sales plummeted. But, as the writer of an editorial in the *New York Times* observed, 'Hell hath no fury like a pesticide scorned.'[16] The food and chemical industries launched a furious counter-attack, claiming that there was little evidence to support the dangerous effects of the chemical and that the media had raised a false alarm, leading to tremendous losses for growers. The well-financed corporate campaign forced the EPA to withdraw the outright ban. The result, however, was something of a draw for the industry and environmentalists. The term 'scare' is still used for the controversy, reflecting the industry's view that it was a scare rather than a real threat. Laws were passed in some states giving agricultural producers a stronger argument in suing the media and celebrities for inciting food-safety scares that cost farmers money.[17] At the same time, the controversy raised concerns about agricultural chemicals, and environmentalists were able to convince Congress to pass other regulations.

Industry groups such as the Midwest Apple Improvement Association now reflect both sides of the argument. While it dismisses the Alar episode as a 'sensationalized story . . . about harmless, nearly non-existent chemical residues on apples', the association expressed views on chemicals quite different from those of other growers. Its website, 'Great Moments in Apple History', proudly explains that the association was organized in 1998 as 'a group dedicated to breeding disease resistant late bloomers to naturally escape' the apple scourges that were traditionally fought with chemicals, a fact, it says, that made 'chemical companies cringe'. It also makes an important point that is not always heard from apple growers: 'Land grant colleges of agriculture are in a bind because increasingly their funding comes from pesticide manufacturers instead of the people through taxation and charitable giving.'[18]

Soviet Apples

The negative influence of corporate capitalism has been an all too familiar pattern in American apple growing. Less well known is the former Soviet Union's role in squelching recognition of the apple's genetic diversity. Although Johann Sievers identified the species *Malus sieversii* growing in Kazakhstan in 1793, it would be another 136 years before another scientist would recognize its genetic relationship to cultivated apples. 'The apple's original home is not definitely known', S. A. Beach wrote in 1905.[19] The mystery was solved in 1929 when Nikolai Vavilov, a Russian plant geneticist on a biological expedition, arrived by mule train at an ancient trading centre along the Silk Road amid the Tian Shan Mountains of Kazakhstan. In Almaty (from the

Russian for 'father of apples'), every ravine and slope he saw was covered with an astonishing variety of wild apple trees bearing large fruit. He soon determined that they were the ancestors of the cultivated sweet apple, and recognized that the area was a treasure trove for apple research and breeding.

Tragically, both Vavilov and his findings would be buried by Soviet ideology. Joseph Stalin's totalitarian regime (1924–53) controlled every aspect of Soviet life, including science. His scientific adviser, Trofim Denisovich Lysenko, denounced genetics and its long-established demonstrations of inherited characteristics as contrary to Communist thought. If the social environment could shape man, as Communists believed they were doing, it followed that plants and animals also evolved through characteristics acquired from their environment, not their ancestors. Although Russia had been in the forefront of genetic science in the first third of the twentieth century, Lysenko's socialist genetics became the basis of Soviet agriculture – and caused devastating food shortages and famine. In the 1940s, scientific geneticists like Vavilov were arrested as traitors. Vavilov ended up in prison in Leningrad, where he starved to death in 1943 during the German siege of the city. After remaining hidden for nearly half a century, his findings finally came to light through the efforts of a Kazakh botanist, Aimak Djangaliev, who had helped Vavilov in Kazakhstan. Narrowly escaping Soviet persecution himself, Djangaliev quietly continued his mentor's study of apples in virtual obscurity in Almaty. As he grew older, he saw the wild forests threatened by the development of ski resorts and mining – a threat that continues today.[20] In the late 1980s he invited a group of U.S. plant scientists to the mountains to tap this vast resource and raise awareness about its importance. In August 1989 a team from the U.S. National Clonal Germplasm Repository arrived in Almaty and began the first of several expeditions there, collecting seeds and scions to study and preserve, to secure the future of the apple.

Apple Activists

In reaction to the corporate domination of the market for apples and other fruits, a grass-roots movement emerged in the 1980s, employing the tactics of political action. One of the more recent groups, Fallen Fruit, an artists' collaborative based in Los Angeles, has mapped neighbourhood fruit trees that overhang public streets and pavements, and urges people to help themselves to this public bounty. One of their posters urges people to 'Plant a fruit tree near your home', and depicts the famous image of the flag being raised by three American soldiers at Iwo Jima during the Second World War. Instead of a flag, however, the soldiers here are planting an apple tree against the backdrop of the urban landscape. The Guerrilla

David Burns, Matias Viegener and Austin Young, Fallen Fruit Collaborative, *Urban Fruit Action*, public billboard series, 2005.

Scrumping apples.

Grafters in San Francisco surreptitiously graft fruit-tree branches on to ornamental trees. In the UK, groups such as Abundance (active in various cities) and the London Orchard Project have organized a return to the old tradition of scrumping fruit. Packs of adults and children have become guerrilla fruit pickers, climbing fences and braving rats, stray dogs and broken bottles to pick apples growing on trees in abandoned gardens. At times, homeowners who cannot reach the fruit in their back gardens call the pickers to help. Some school groups do it as a fund-raising project, selling the fruit to restaurants and using the money for their school. Although scrumping – that is, picking without permission – is still illegal in England, the last reported prosecution, according to the National Archives, was in 1829.[21]

eleven

Apples Today and Tomorrow

pples are not the largest fruit crop in the world. Not even counting tomatoes (which are botanically fruits, although not commonly considered as such), the apple is in fourth place after bananas, oranges and grapes.[1] But apples are the most ubiquitous and well-adapted fruit, and are grown nearly everywhere. China and the USA have by far the biggest lead, and, according to agricultural reports in 2010, many other countries have significant apple crops, some in surprising places, at least to Western minds. The third largest producer is Turkey. The fourth is Italy, a place where one usually thinks of tomatoes before apples; despite the many delicious French tarts and German strudels, Italy is the largest apple producer in Europe. The Italian word for apple, *mela*, is derived from the Latin *malus*, although most of the Italian crop is grown in the country's northern section, where German is also spoken. France is seventh in apple production, after Poland (fifth) and India (sixth), ahead of Germany (fourteenth) and far ahead of the UK, which ranks 38th out of 93 countries on the list.

Yet the demand for apples is dropping in both Europe and America, and growers throughout the world face an uncertain future. The cultivation of today's apples is continuing to move in two opposite directions: big commercial producers, who dominate the global industry, and small, local orchards, many of which are growing heirloom varieties. Each approach raises questions about its own viability in a highly competitive market, and about the future of the

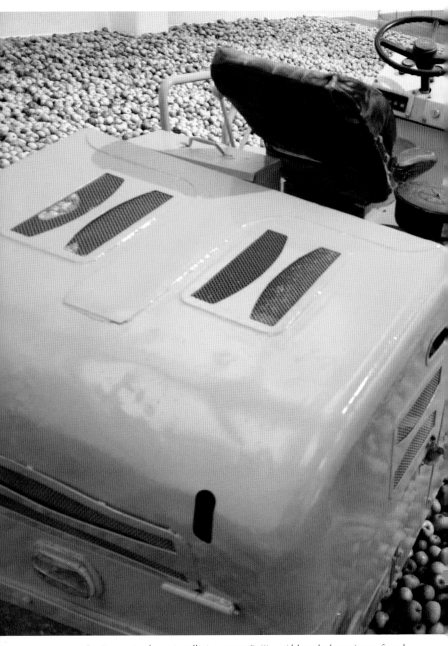

Gu Dexin, Apple art installation, 2012, Beijing. Although the artist preferred
not to provide an interpretation for his work, it is a fitting tribute to China's
role as the world's largest apple producer.

apple itself. The questions are far-reaching, and include the financial and environmental cost of pesticides, genetic breeding, and the quality and biodiversity of the fruit. There are no simple answers, but there are many approaches to finding solutions.

To Spray or Not to Spray

In 1912 Laura Ingalls Wilder, who would become known for her best-selling *Little House on the Prairie* books for children (1932–43), wrote a column for the local newspaper about her apple farm in the Ozark Mountains of Missouri. Although agricultural sprays of different sorts were common at the time, Wilder never used them. Instead, she mixed wood ashes into the soil, which discouraged woolly aphids, and allowed her chickens and wild quail to peck around the trees, keeping the borers away.[2]

While country gardeners may benefit from following Wilder's advice, her methods unfortunately seem like wishful thinking for the massive scale of apple growing today. Most commercial apple growers, both large and small, use pesticides – and most would be happy to stop using them, because the escalating costs of chemicals cut into their profits. Like the 'Just Say No' anti-drugs campaign of the 1980s, there is no easy way to stop the use of pesticides, because apple orchards provide a constant feast for insects and bacterial and fungal diseases. While the demand for chemical-free apples is increasing, the general public, accustomed to unblemished fruit in supermarkets, has little tolerance for apples that reveal even the harmless spots of untreated fruit. Yet a number of small orchardists remain undaunted. Elizabeth Ryan, owner of Breezy Hill Orchard and Cider Mill in upstate New York, has suggested an 'ugly apple' promotion, similar to the ugly tomato campaign in the USA that encouraged shoppers to buy misshapen heirlooms with more flavour than perfectly round ones.[3] Ryan operates one of an increasing number of small orchards that practise integrated methods of pest management, strictly limiting chemicals and using alternatives targeted to specific insects.

Spraying at an organic apple orchard in New Zealand. Certain plant-based
and 'natural' mineral insecticides are considered organic.

Organic and heirloom orchards are also increasing, but their
apples are not all free of pesticides. Organic methods, which may use
certain plant-based insecticides, such as rotenone, can kill good as
well as harmful insects. Ezekiel Goodband, the heirloom orchardist
at Scott Farm in Vermont, prefers sprays targeted to specific pests,
along with a variety of alternative methods that work just as well
with other insects.[4] One of the worst pests, the apple maggot, riddles
fruit with brown trails of burrowing larvae. But the female looking
for a good place to lay her eggs is fooled by big, red ersatz apples
covered with a sticky material known as Tangletrap, which traps and
kills her. One trap can protect a whole tree. 'The less I bother the
trees, the happier they are', Goodband says.[5]

Spraying the trees is not enough for some conventional orchardists,
who place herbicide strips between the trees to kill weeds and grass
that compete for nutrients in the soil. Goodband, however, believes
that they cause the tree's roots to become 'pot-bound', that is, confined

to a small area around the tree. Like potted plants, they then require more fertilizer. He describes his trees as 'free-range', because their roots are free to 'root' around in the soil, like pigs and other free-range farmyard animals.[6]

Michael Phillips of Heartsong Farm in New Hampshire was determined to avoid all pesticides, even the 'natural' sulphur and copper sprays permitted in certified organic orchards in the U.S. But it was not easy, particularly fighting off the apple-tree borer, which can kill a tree if undetected. 'I lost fifty apple trees getting my degree in borers', he admits.[7] He eventually found natural solutions: neem oil and other sprays made from liquid fish fertilizer, along with horsetail and stinging nettles, which he plants around the trees. Both of these wild plants are high in silica, which deters fungal diseases.

Phillips has also tackled the problem of declining honeybee populations. Each year since 2006, North American bee-keepers have lost about a third of their honeybee colonies to a disease known as colony collapse disorder. Although the cause has not been absolutely determined, tests on bees have revealed large concentrations of different pesticides used on many types of crops. Phillips has switched to native mason bees and bumblebees, the ones that early American colonists ignored. 'Honeybees are like bankers', he says. 'They work 9 to 5, and only when it's 60 degrees [F; 15.5°C]. Bumblebees and mason bees work from first light until dark, and pollinate all the female parts of a flower, so all the seeds take.'[8] He is also bagging his apples, as the Japanese do, not to create works of art, but to keep destructive insects out. Such labour-intensive methods are impractical for large commercial growers, but Phillips, the author of *The Holistic Orchard: Tree Fruits and Berries the Biological Way* (2011), wants to share information with other small orchardists and domestic gardeners in the hope that they will increase in number and reduce the use of pesticides.

Old is New

While Victorian plant explorers were discovering exotic plants and foods around the world in the late nineteenth century, some people back home in England were becoming nostalgic for the traditional taste of English apples. The arrival of American apples in nearly every shop window led horticulturists and gardeners to discover and start growing lost English varieties once again. The same impulse has seized apple lovers in the USA today, particularly in New England, where American apple growing began. Confronted with mass-market fruit, this new breed of explorers and orchardists is searching for old varieties at home and reviving those that are nearly extinct.

John Bunker puts up 'Wanted Alive' posters for lost varieties in Maine, and now grows more than 200, some of which are more than 200 years old, at his Super Chilly Farm in the tiny town of Palermo.[9] Goodband grows more than 90 heirloom varieties at Scott Farm, an orchard with a unique history. The property, in Dummerston in southeastern Vermont, was the home of Rudyard Kipling from 1892 to 1896. Kipling built a home there for himself and his American bride and christened it 'Naulakha', a Hindi word meaning 'jewel beyond price'. During their short residence there, he wrote *The Jungle Book* and *Captains Courageous* and began *Kim* and the *Just So Stories*. The orchard was established as a family farm in 1915 and operated for several generations before going into decline. The Landmark Trust USA, the American branch of the UK organization, acquired Naulakha in 1993 and restored the house and orchard.[10] Goodband arrived in 2001 with his collection of heirloom scions, which he grafted on to 5,000 old trees.

Antique apples grown on old southern plantations are also being revived and shared with new heirloom enthusiasts. Creighton Lee Calhoun Jr, the author of an updated edition of *Old Southern Apples* (2011), a directory of 2,000 varieties, grows 300 different kinds of

overleaf: Ananas Reinettes, a pineapple-flavoured heirloom growing at Scott Farm, 2013.

heirloom apple on his farm, Horne Creek Living Historical Farm in Pinnacle, North Carolina, and has donated hundreds to young growers.[11] When the apple historian Tom Burford, author of *Apples of North America: 192 Exceptional Varieties for Gardeners, Growers and Cooks* (2013), retired from his family nursery in Virginia, he donated his collection of 200 heirlooms to another orchardist. Keeping these old varieties alive will do more than provide good eating for local customers.

As climate change brings warmer spring temperatures to northern apple trees, reducing the number of cold days (necessary to produce blossom and fruit), the heat-tolerant southern varieties could provide critical replacements for northern nurseries. They also could be life-savers for the economies of developing countries that cannot afford their own breeding programmes, according to Kevin Hauser, the author of *Growing Apples in the Tropics: The Complete Guide to Growing Apples Where They're Not Supposed To* (2011). Hauser owns Kuffel Creek Apple Nursery in Riverside, southern California, where he specializes in growing apples that are suited to hot inland climates. After 200 years of selective breeding, old southern apples, he explains, are well adapted to heat, humidity and disease, and could open up industries in tropical Africa and the Caribbean.[12]

Most heirloom growers are not impressed by the latest cultivars, such as the celebrated Honeycrisp/Honeycrunch, and do not aspire to supermarket status for their own apples. Many of the old varieties are too fragile to ship and do not keep their flavour in long-term storage – showing why they were abandoned by conventional growers aiming for the mass market. 'We try to sell everything by Christmas', Goodband says.[13] Fortunately, the growing popularity of heirloom varieties has encouraged some large apple nurseries to carry the trees. Stark Brothers, for example, now sells several heirloom trees, including Cox's Orange Pippin and Ben Davis. A mega-producer of conventionally grown apples, Stemilt in Washington State is also the nation's largest supplier of organic tree fruit. 'It's often the smallholding farmer and homesteader who leads the way', David Buchanan explains. It is unrealistic to think that local apples will replace mass marketing, he says, but 'they deserve their place at the table.'[14] In countries like England where imports have greatly outnumbered locally grown apples, the growers of conventionally grown local fruit also need a place in supermarkets, or eventually all apples will be imported.[15]

Back to the Future

Conventional apple breeders are banking on strategies quite different from those that have helped heirloom and organic orchards to break away from pesticides. The most promising alternatives lie in the apple itself, in its unlimited genetic possibilities to develop varieties that are resistant to insects and disease, as well as highly nutritious and tasty. One of the amazing things the research team discovered in the forest of Almaty, Khazakhstan, was that most of the wild apples were relatively free from insect damage, compared to the fruit of commercial orchards. Since the U.S. team's first trip there, in 1989, scientists from a number of countries have visited and collected samples of the diverse varieties to study and preserve for the future. Philip Forsline, a horticulturalist with the U.S. Department of Agriculture (USDA), made several expeditions in the 1990s and brought back 140,000 seeds and 900 scions to the USDA's Plant Genetic Resources Unit in Geneva, New York, home to the world's most extensive collection of apple varieties and relatives.[16] The seeds provide a broad base of genetic information, and the scions have produced a living orchard for breeding better apples.

The Geneva station had started collecting data about apples a century earlier, when the U.S. government began to create federally funded agricultural experiment stations in every state. In the late 1880s controlling pests and diseases was the priority, and chemical pesticides were seen as the answer. Although they were promoted throughout commercial and private apple orchards, the breeding of disease-resistant apples also slowly began, at times quite by accident. In 1907 Charles Crandall, a horticulturalist at the University of Illinois, began crossing different species of crab apple with commercial apples. He was not looking for disease-resistance particularly, but in 1943 another horticulturalist discovered that some of the trees created by Crandall's crosses had survived a severe apple scab epidemic that had defoliated most of the other unsprayed trees. Since then, breeders at several other research stations in the USA and throughout the world have continued to experiment with disease-resistant crosses, and have released more than 1,000 apple cultivars resistant to apple scab, powdery mildew and fireblight. The resistance of crab apples to scab, however, has lessened over the years as the pathogen has evolved. Many varieties, including the popular Japanese flowering crab, *Malus floribunda*, which was the original disease-resistant species used in cross-breedings, still depend upon several fungicide treatments a year.[17] Today's horticulturalists are armed with both advances in genetic science and thousands of apple species from the ancient forests of Central Asia, the immense warehouse of unexplored genetic possibilities for the apple's future. Working with huge collections in Geneva, as well as England's National Fruit Collection and Germany's apple gene bank, they have a vast reserve and the tools to deepen the shallow gene pool of cloned supermarket apples.

Genetically Modified Apples

Developing disease-resistant varieties requires enormous outlay of time and money, making it impossible to predict when or if the apple industry will ever abandon or significantly reduce the use of pesticides. The Winecrisp apple, which carries a gene for resistance to scab, was developed without genetic engineering, but, like most apple breeding, it took twenty years before it was ready for release to nurseries, in 2009. Just looking for a tasty apple among thousands of trees planted as trial seedlings is like 'sifting through dirt for diamonds', according to David Bedford, the University of Minnesota's chief apple breeder, who tastes about 500 to 600 apples a day.[18]

Although many of the most famous apple varieties originated centuries ago as chance seedlings, it is rare today for a tree that sprouts

Malus Floribunda, botanical print, 1845. This beautiful crab apple initially showed resistance to apple scab, but, along with other crab-apple varieties, still depends upon frequent fungicide treatments.

up on its own to make it to the commercial market. Fewer than a dozen have made it in the past 50 years. Genetic analysis of apple parents to predict the characteristics of the next generation is much faster than waiting years to find out if a new cultivar looks and tastes good. But the technique is still relatively rare and expensive – and may not be as reliable for determining flavour as an experienced breeder with one good bite. Genetic engineers can also lift a desired gene from virtually any living organism and transfer it to almost any other organism. They have spliced genes from the Cecropia moth into apple plants to provide protection from fire blight.[19]

But public resistance to or outright refusal to buy genetically modified foods, even those produced without inter-species transfer, was dramatically demonstrated in the overwhelmingly negative reaction to the relatively innocent GM apple that does not turn brown when sliced. In 2012 a company based in British Columbia sought U.S. approval for selling Arctic apples in America. The new product contains a synthetic gene that sharply reduces the enzyme responsible for the flesh turning brown when exposed to the air. The gene did

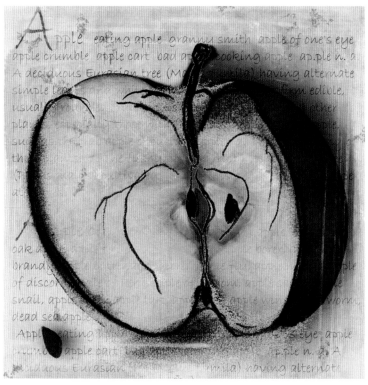

Anthony Hammond, sliced apple drawing, 2001. Sliced apples turn brown,
a fact that has led to the introduction of a controversial GM apple that
keeps its white flesh when cut.

not come from another species, but was derived from the apple itself. Nevertheless, both industry and anti-GM groups protested loudly at the public hearing. Industry opponents worried that a GM apple would taint the fruit's reputation as a healthy food. The head of the anti-GM group asked, 'Is it a rotten apple that looks fresh?', raising the age-old suspicion, just as Shakespeare had, about 'a goodly apple rotten at the core'.[20] The company representative answered that if an Arctic apple rotted, it would turn brown as a warning that it was not good to eat, but the hundreds of opponents at the hearing were not convinced. Altering genes for cosmetic effect seems frivolous – just brushing cut apples with lemon juice or wrapping them in plastic film will retard browning – but even the stronger arguments for genetically engineering apples as an alternative to using pesticides are still a matter of great debate.

Controlled Cultivars

Apple breeders and growers have much greater concerns about their cultivars than the tendency of slices to brown. The best-sellers are often the victims of their own popularity, for reasons beyond the breeders' control. The fruit can lose its best qualities if growers plant the trees in an unsuitable climate or soil, or pick the apples too early. The Red Delicious was once truly delicious, but over the hundred years or so since it was discovered, it has become a different apple. Even before storage and long-distance shipping had taken their toll, it was often propagated by sports, mutations branching from the same tree. The ones with the reddest fruit were selected, regardless of taste.

Today's apples, branded, patented and trademarked, are 'more like the apple on my computer than in the school lunchbox I once carried', the *New Yorker* writer John Seabrook observed.[21] Unlike apples, computers do not reproduce and change. Patents and trademarks provide licensing fees and royalties, but breeders are also concerned about the integrity of their brands. Many have developed management strategies similar to those of companies that manufacture rather than grow their products. Honeycrisp/Honeycrunch, heralded as the iPod of the apple because of its industry-wide success, generated millions of dollars from tree sales to help pay for a supercomputer – one of the world's fastest – for its creator, the University of Minnesota.[22] Researchers are now using it for other cutting-edge technology in the hope of making new discoveries and revenues for the university. But Honeycrisp was sold under open release, meaning that any grower could grow it anywhere and however they wanted. The quality varied widely, and the university's revenue ended once its patent for the variety expired, in 2008.

For its new cultivar, SweeTango, the university wanted to control the quality of the brand and create a longer revenue stream. It established a consortium that retains the right to decide who can grow the variety, how they grow it and for how long it can be grown. The growers cannot sell the apples directly to a supermarket, but must sell them to the consortium, which does the marketing.[23] Dozens of other commercial varieties, most of them grown outside the USA, are similarly produced and marketed in clubs, with growing access limited to club members.[24] Small orchards, however, are excluded from growing the latest varieties if they cannot afford the fees required for club membership.[25]

The Future of the Apple

Mass-marketing methods and genetic engineering have raised fears that the apple will be transformed from a fresh fruit into a processed, industrialized product. The vision of the apple's future as treated slices in plastic bags has already taken shape in a number of products. Packages of so-called ready-to-eat apples, sliced and coated with an edible film, have been available in school cafeterias, grocery shops and fast-food restaurants since the 1980s. Kept under refrigeration, they can last for two or three weeks without turning brown. The technique has been adopted for many other fruits and vegetables,

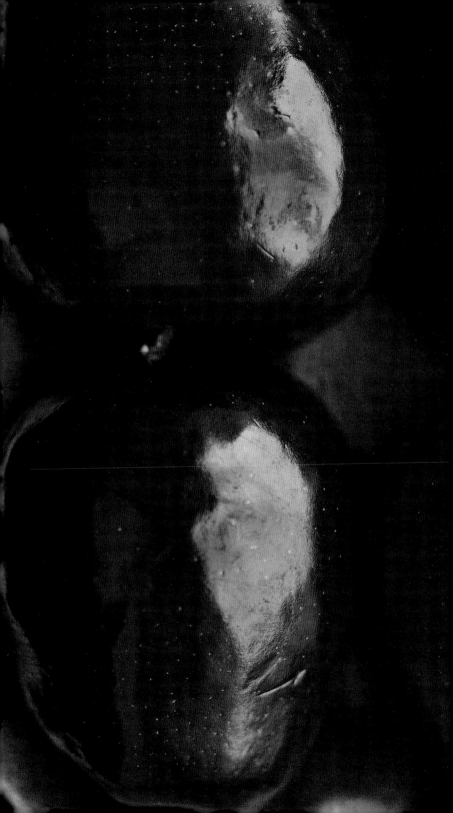

with the exception of two that also brown easily when cut – bananas and avocados – which have so far eluded a successful application.

A few more recent apple products have been created and marketed as healthy alternatives to snack foods and desserts, but without apple flavour. Grapples, apples infused with sweet grape juice and sealed in plastic packages, are being sold in the U.S. with the slogan 'Crunches like an apple. Tastes like a grape.' Even the pronunciation of the name – 'Say Grape-L' – obscures the apple. McDonald's Apple Dippers, packages of sliced and peeled apples with a sweet caramel dipping sauce, are deconstructed candy apples that also do not bode well for the apple's future as a fresh fruit. But to paraphrase Mark Twain upon seeing his own obituary, reports of the apple's death are premature. The apple's more popular competitors, the banana and the orange, face more serious threats from virulent diseases that have been destroying commercial crops. Their best hope for survival, particularly for the sterile, seedless banana, could be genetic engineering.[26] No such weakling, the apple has proved itself a rugged survivor. Even the commercial varieties carry a secret weapon, the infinite ability of their seeds to adapt, producing new trees that can overcome both disease and agribusiness.

There will always be apples, but what kind of apples can we expect to find in the near future? The Red Delicious, the bête noire of apple aficionados, may be giving way to newer varieties with more taste and crunch, but the economics of global marketing will probably always favour apples that are cheaper to grow, store and ship. Will the rich culture of the apple survive as bland apples take us further away from the stories that made them magical? In 1998 Frank Browning optimistically predicted that people will always want to touch and eat something real. Happily, he still seems to be right. The continued popularity of pick-your-own apple orchards, the growth of farmers' markets, the lust for locally grown food and the greater environmental awareness of pesticides and the desire to reverse the

Red Delicious apples in a plastic package.

Organic apple fruit stamp. The demand for chemical-free fruit is increasing.

damage they cause are all anthems for real apples. Small orchards will no doubt continue to struggle. Many seasonal market operators believe they cannot attract customers with apples alone. They also offer cider doughnuts, apple pies, gifts, hayrides, Halloween events and wassailing festivals. But the apple is at the centre of it all. 'People aren't coming out here to pick apples because they need food', one orchardist remarked.[27] They come for something they can't find in the supermarket. Apple trees in our back gardens and farmers' markets strike a deeper chord in our cultural consciousness, a longing to experience a sense of place, time and vibrant taste that has nearly been lost.

Apple Varieties

There is in the Apple a vast range of flavours and textures, and for those who adventure in the realm of taste, a field for much hopeful voyaging.

EDWARD BUNYARD, *The Anatomy of Dessert*

As Bunyard explains so well, the apple offers a wonderful variety for eating, cooking, growing and cider making. This directory includes just a small sample of the thousands of heirloom and modern varieties that can be found by those who choose to look for them. Please note that the flavours described here may not be the same unless you are biting into a fresh apple. I confess that I have not tasted them all, and I am indebted to the consensus of ex-perienced apple growers and lovers, many of whom are listed in the websites at the back of this book. The heirlooms are rarely available outside speciality orchards, but home gardeners can generally find the trees in online nursery listings. Check your local growing conditions for compatibility.

Ambrosia

Discovered in an orchard of Jonagold trees in British Columbia, Canada, in the early 1990s, this is one of the rare chance seedlings in recent history that have made their way to today's commercial market. The red and yellow fruit is low in acid and, when sliced, is said to turn brown more slowly than other apples do.

Ambrosia.

Ananas Reinette

The name of this heirloom apple means 'pineapple princess' in French, although it was first documented in the Netherlands in 1821. Reinettes, established in France in the 1500s, are a class of yellow or green apple that was made into desserts and considered 'fit for a princess'. This one has russet 'freckles' over a bright yellow skin, and an aromatic pineapple flavour that develops late in the season.

Ashmead's Kernel

A famous heirloom from the early 1700s, this apple is one of a few English varieties that also grow well in North America. Greenish-yellow with a dull russet skin, it has a sharp, sweet flavour that lends itself to desserts, cider and juice. 'Kernel' refers to an apple grown from a seedling, and this one was originally raised by a Dr Ashmead in Gloucester.

Baldwin

Once America's most popular apple, the Baldwin succumbed to the forces of nature and the pressures of the national market. Discovered as a seedling in about 1740 in Massachusetts, it was an exceptionally hardy, disease-resistant apple, prized for pies and cider. In 1934 severe spring frosts killed off many of the New England orchards, and, rather than being replanted, the trees were replaced by new cultivars considered more commercially viable.

Belle de Boskoop

This mid-nineteenth century introduction from Boskoop, the Netherlands, is considered the premier apple for strudel. A large green-gold fruit, dotted with orange and russet, it has firm, crisp flesh that holds its shape in baking and also makes a thick sauce. Its sweet—tart flavour mellows after harvest, which can last into December.

Belle de Boskoop.

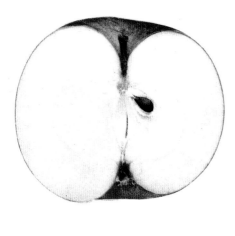

Blue Pearmain.

Blue Pearmain

Pearmain apples are pear-like in their shape or taste. This New England heirloom almost glows with a bluish tint when ripe. Its flavour and texture are recommended for baking, although Henry Thoreau loved to eat the apples straight from the tree: 'I do not refuse the Blue Pearmain', he wrote in his essay 'Wild Apples' of 1862. 'I fill my pockets on each side; and as I retrace my steps in the frosty eve, being perhaps four or five miles from home, I eat one first from this side, and then from that, to keep my balance.'

Braeburn.

Braeburn

This streaky red-orange fruit was the first of a new wave that brought some variety to bland supermarket apples. It was discovered as a chance seedling in a New Zealand orchard in 1952. Of unknown parentage, it is thought to be a cross between Granny Smith and Lady Hamilton apples, both of which were grown at the orchard. It was later commercially grown at Braeburn Orchards, also in New Zealand, for which it was named.

Bramley's Seedling

Prized by English cooks, this is the most popular culinary apple in the UK and one of the few heirlooms that survives as a major variety in today's commercial market. It was raised as a seedling in a Nottinghamshire cottage garden from 1809 to 1813, introduced as a commercial variety in 1865 and recognized as an outstanding apple by the Royal Horticultural Society in 1893.

Bramley.

Calville Blanc d'Hiver.

Cameo.

Calville Blanc d'Hiver

A lumpy-looking apple with a Champagne flavour, this seventeenth-century French heirloom ('Calville's white winter apple') has a gourmet reputation. It is the fruit of choice for tarte Tatin, a classic dessert with a topping of caramelized apples.

Cameo

Discovered in Washington State in 1987, this chance seedling may be the offspring of two famous parents, Red Delicious and Golden Delicious, which were grown near by. Its shape is similar to the Red Delicious, but its bright red skin streaked over yellow reflects both parents.

Chenango Strawberry

With its blushing skin and conical shape, this apple looks something like a giant strawberry, and it has the aroma and slight taste of that delicate fruit. Although it has been around since 1854, when it was first recorded in Chenango County in Central New York State, it does not like extremely cold temperatures. It is also self-sterile and needs a pollination partner near by.

Claygate Pearmain

John Braddick of Claygate, Surrey, found this pear-shaped apple growing in a hedge in about 1821 and named it after his village. Its firm, juicy flesh made it a popular Victorian dessert apple, and it received a First Class Certificate from the Royal Horticultural Society in 1921.

Cortland.

Cortland

This big apple has been a mainstay of American kitchens since it was created in 1915 at the Agricultural Experiment Station in Geneva, New York. A cross between McIntosh and Ben Davis apples, it was known for years as the premier baked apple, but knowledgeable cooks prefer harder varieties that keep their shape. It is now promoted for staying white when sliced into salads.

Costard apples

In Shakespeare's time, 'costard' was another word for 'apple' and a slang term for a man's head. Costard was a comic figure in *Love's Labour's Lost*, and a costermonger is an apple seller. The term may derive from the French, dating back to the Norman invasion, when the French introduced many apple trees to Britain. Heirloom costard apples, such as the Wotton Costard, from the orchard of a seventeenth-century estate near Wotton, Gloucestershire, are still available and are excellent for cooking.

Cox.

Cox's Orange Pippin

Raised by Richard Cox, a retired brewer from Buckinghamshire, in about 1825, this variety is still one of England's favourite eating apples. It has a distinctive orange-red colour and complex flavours, yet has been susceptible to fungal diseases when grown in North America. Several strains and hybrids, which all bear the Cox name, have shown greater resistance to disease.

Crispin

Formerly known as Mutsu, this green apple was developed in Japan in the 1930s as a cross between the Golden Delicious and Japanese Indo apples. It is bigger than most apples, has a sprightly taste and can be baked or eaten fresh.

Dolgo

Native to northern Russia, this hardy crab-apple variety was brought to the USA in 1897 to grow in the harsh climate of South Dakota.

Longer than it is wide, it is named for the Russian word for 'long'. It is sweeter than most crab apples, with a zesty flavour similar to that of cranberries, and is used for jellies and cider. The vigorous trees bloom profusely and can reach 12 m (40 ft) in height.

Duchess of Oldenburg

This Russian variety, brought to the USA in the 1830s, thrives in cold climates and is also said to be resistant to apple scab. Pale yellow with splashes and stripes of pinkish red, it is an attractive apple and a flavourful one for cooking.

Empire

Two of the most popular apples, Red Delicious and McIntosh, are the parents of this brilliant-red variety. Named for the Empire state of New York, it was created at New York's Agricultural Experiment Station in Geneva, in partnership with Cornell University, and introduced in 1966.

Empire.

Esopus Spitzenberg.

Esopus Spitzenburg

Thomas Jefferson loved this spicy apple but had a difficult time growing it in the hot climate of his Monticello orchards in Virginia. It came from Esopus, a cool, mountainous region in New York's Hudson Valley, and had presumably been planted there in the early eighteenth century by a Dutch settler named Spitzenburg.

EverCrisp

Released in 2012, this variety was developed by the Midwest Apple Improvement Association from a cross between another pair of market superstars, Fuji and Honeycrisp/Honeycrunch. The name refers to both its crunchy texture and its long-keeping quality.

Flower of Kent

This is the legendary variety of apple from Isaac Newton's tree. Whether or not one actually fell on his head, inspiring his theory of gravity, its culinary qualities must have inspired cooking in the Newton household.

Fuji.

Fuji

A sweet, crisp apple with dense flesh, Fuji was developed by Japanese breeders in the late 1930s and has become a multicultural phenomenon. It is a cross between two American cultivars, Red Delicious and Ralls Genet, the latter introduced by a Frenchman to Thomas Jefferson in the late eighteenth century. Fuji is enormously popular, but critics fear that some supplies may have the same fate as the Red Delicious: becoming overproduced, overly red and overly sweet.

Gala

Developed in New Zealand in the 1930s and now one of the most popular apples in the U.S. and UK, Gala is a descendant of two generations of Delicious apples. Its parents are Golden Delicious and Kidd's Orange Red, a hybrid of Red Delicious and Cox's Orange Pippin. The Delicious influence has tempered the more pronounced Cox flavour.

Golden Delicious.

Golden Delicious

When Clarence Stark bought this apple tree from a farmer who had discovered it in West Virginia in 1914, he considered it so valuable that he placed it in a tall cage, secured with a burglar alarm. Although it sounds like a cousin to Stark's most famous find, the Red Delicious, the Golden Delicious is a variety all its own. Its mild, sweet flavour and pleasing round shape have made it one of the most popular apples on the world market.

Granny Smith

A granny actually propagated this apple in southeast Australia in the nineteenth century: Maria Ann Smith, known in her old age as 'Granny'. Later growers made it famous, but Granny's name stuck. It became the first popular supermarket apple that was not red. Tart, but not sour, and long-lasting in storage, it has become one of the best-selling varieties on the commercial market. Recent studies have shown that it has more nutrients than most red apples.

Gravenstein.

Gravenstein

Possibly originating in Denmark or Germany in the seventeenth century, Gravenstein is still a favourite variety in northern Europe, but many critics believe that it reaches perfection in northern California. Russian settlers in the nineteenth century planted it in Sonoma County, California, where the soil and climate have nourished both fine wines and apples. Fans of Gravenstein rave about its crisp, tender flesh, sweet–tart juice and intense aroma. While it has lost ground to mass-market apples, it is enjoying a renaissance in heirloom orchards.

Harrison Cider Apple

Celebrated in America throughout the nineteenth century, this variety produced a dark, rich cider. It originated in New Jersey, but was thought to be extinct until it was rediscovered by a New Jersey man in 1976. Cider connoisseurs continue to sing its praises, both for its distinctive taste and for its resistance to apple scab and rot.

Hewe's Virginia Crab

Although Thomas Jefferson is known as an apple connoisseur, he concentrated on growing only a few varieties at his Monticello estate in Virginia. This was one of his favourites for cider. The fruit is small and the colour a dull red, but the firm, acidic flesh adds a great depth of flavour to cider.

Holstein

One of the few good things to have come out of First World War Germany, this apple was discovered in the Holstein region of the country in 1918. It may have grown as a chance seedling of Cox's Orange Pippin (from a core dropped by a British soldier, one might imagine). It yields delicious orange-yellow juice with a slight pineapple flavour.

Honeycrisp (Honeycrunch)

A contemporary superstar with outstanding flavour, crispness and juiciness, this cultivar was bred at the University of Minnesota and was nearly overlooked. One of its parents was most likely the Keepsake apple (little known outside Minnesota); the other remains a mystery, identified only by a number, apparently discarded during research trials. Honeycrisp, which is known in Europe as Honeycrunch, overcame its humble beginnings to achieve unrivalled success on the commercial market. By 2006 it had become so famous that it was selected as one of the top 25 innovations that changed the world, a list that included Google.

Hubbardston Nonesuch

As its name reveals, this was the pride of Hubbardston, Massachusetts, in the late 1700s, an apple without compare. Today it grows only in heirloom orchards, where growers are preserving its appealing qualities. It is a large apple with an unusually small core and crisp, sweet flesh, tasty for eating and cider making.

Idared

Woody Guthrie sang an old American folksong about a woman named Ida Red, but the 'Ida' of this variety refers to the cultivar's birth in Idaho in 1942. It was a cross between the well-known Jonathan apple and the less well-known Wagener. It keeps its shape during cooking, making it a favourite for baked apples and pies.

Indian Magic

Cooking with crab apples is a lost art, but signs of its revival can be seen at farmers' markets, where this variety is appearing in jars of home-made jam. Like most crab-apple trees today, it is primarily known for its ornamental value. Its red buds open in spring to rose-pink flowers that develop elongated, red-orange fruits.

Idared.

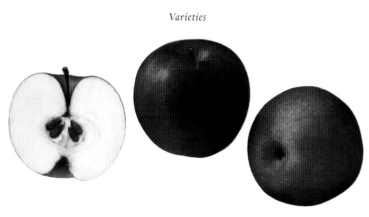

Jonathan.

Jazz

Launched in the early twenty-first century, this newcomer is one of New Zealand's latest developments, a cross between two of its other highly popular cultivars, Royal Gala and Braeburn. Now grown in many parts of the world, it has become a popular variety, known for its dense, tart–sweet, crunchy flesh.

Jonathan

An early nineteenth-century variety, Jonathan became one of the best known and most widespread of American apples. Its offspring, Jonagold and Jonamac, have become almost as popular. Both were developed in Geneva, New York, as crosses with two other classic American varieties. Jonagold, released in 1968, was a cross of Jonathan with Golden Delicious; Jonamac came about in 1972 through a Jonathan–McIntosh cross.

Kanzi

A new European development, Kanzi originated in Belgium as a cross between Gala and Braeburn apples. A bright red fruit, it has become one of the most commonly grown varieties in Europe, and has entered the U.S. market, particularly in speciality shops.

Kiku

In 1990 an Italian apple grower touring an orchard in Japan noticed bright red apples with an intensely sweet flavour growing as a sport (mutation) on a Fuji apple tree. He bought the rights to the apple and began growing it in Italy. Primarily grown there, it was introduced to select growers in the U.S. in 2010 as a 'supersweet' apple. On a scale of tart to sweet, Kiku apples are considered the sweetest.

King Luscious

As its name promises, this apple is huge and juicy. Some have described it as 'hulking'. It grows on a relatively small tree and was discovered as a seedling in North Carolina in the 1930s. Unlike many oversized fruits, it has good texture and flavour. One or two can make an excellent pie.

Kingston Black

The village of Kingston is in Somerset, a prime apple-growing county, and was home to this popular apple of the nineteenth century. With its bitter-sharp juice, it was a premier cider apple. Today's heirloom cider makers in the UK and U.S. are using it once again, capturing its distinctive taste as a single-vintage cider.

Lady Alice

Washington State, the leading commercial apple producer in the USA, is not usually known for raising chance seedlings, but this variety is an exception. Discovered on a farm there in 1978, it was truly by chance. The farmer accidentally cut into an apple tree with his equipment, and over the next 25 years a new tree grew from the base of the original. Named in memory of the founder of the Washington orchard that propagated it, it made its debut in 2013.

Lady Apple

This little fruit is said to be the oldest known variety of apple, and was grown by the ancient Romans. Like many apples called 'lady', it is quite small – two bites and it is gone. It was an old-fashioned treat, dropped into a Christmas stocking, roasted along with meat or used as a garnish. Bowls of these highly aromatic apples served in Victorian times as a room freshener, to mask unpleasant odours.

Lamb Abbey Pearmain

Like Bramley's Seedling, this variety grew from a seed planted in an English garden two centuries ago. In this case, the garden was in the village of Lamb Abbey in Kent, and the seed is said to have come from an American Newtown Pippin apple. The Lamb Abbey Pearmain – small, with an intense sweet–tart pineapple flavour – became a coveted dessert apple. Heirloom orchards have kept the trees growing for enjoyment today.

Liberty

One of the pioneering disease-resistant apples, Liberty was created by 'inoculating' a Macoun apple with another variety shown to be immune to the deadly scourge of apple scab. The process began in New York in 1955, but the apple was not introduced to the public until 1978. The name reflects the quest to free growers from endless spraying.

McIntosh

John McIntosh, a British Loyalist during the American Revolution, left the colonies to resettle in Ottawa, Canada. There he discovered the apple tree that would bear his name and become known as a classic American (or, more accurately, North American) variety. It is one of the first apples to reach the market in early autumn, but it is a treat that does not last long: it must be eaten within a few weeks, as its crisp texture soon turns soft.

Macoun

A cross between the McIntosh and Jersey Black varieties, Macoun was created in New York but named in honour of W. T. Macoun, a Canadian breeder. Although it has been grown for nearly a century, it has never achieved the fame of its parent McIntosh. Somewhat difficult to grow and store, Macouns are not widely available, but devoted fans seek them out for their sweet, tangy flavour.

Newtown Pippin

Most American apples originated as seeds from European transplants during the colonial era, but this was one of the first to make the reverse trip back to the homeland, where it made quite a splash. It dates to 1730, and was raised from a seedling (pippin) in America's first commercial nursery in Newtown, now part of New York City.

Macoun.

These were the days when apples were prized more for taste than for looks, and the greenish Newtown Pippin with its piney aroma was celebrated by a number of eighteenth- and nineteenth-century celebrities, from Thomas Jefferson and Benjamin Franklin to Queen Victoria. Ignored for most of the twentieth century, it is making an appearance once again in New York parks and heirloom nurseries.

Norfolk Beefing

'Beefing' may make this variety sound like a massive apple, but the term is more likely a corruption of 'biffin', an old English word for a dried, flattened apple (and indeed it is also known as Norfolk Biffin). The apple was first recorded in Norfolk in 1807. The medium-to-large fruit with dark purple, red-flushed skin is still used primarily for cooking and drying. It keeps well, and sweetens with age.

Northern Spy

Whoever came up with the saying 'As American as apple pie' was probably thinking of this apple. In fact, its original name may have been 'Northern Pie'. A clear yellow fruit with red tints, it was discovered in a New York orchard in about 1800, and has been prized ever since for its long-keeping qualities.

Paula Red

A grower discovered this tree in his McIntosh orchard in Michigan in 1960 and named it after his wife, Pauline. It is probably a sport of the McIntosh, but it has its own appealing taste, which has been compared to that of strawberries. Like McIntosh, it softens early in storage and cooking but makes delicious apple sauce.

Pink Lady

This pink-tinged variety was bred in Australia in the 1970s, and by 1996 more than a million trees were planted there. Propagated largely for export, it is now grown in many other countries and sold all over the world. A cross of Golden Delicious and Lady Williams apples, it has a high sugar content that has made it a popular supermarket apple. Its success has led to it becoming known as 'Queen of Australian Apples'.

Red Astrachan

Like the Duchess of Oldenburg, this apple is thought to be of Russian lineage, albeit without the royal title. Swedish immigrants brought it to England and America in the mid-nineteenth century. It ripens early but does not ship well, characteristics that have pushed it out of a larger market, but its tart juiciness is still savoured by those who have sampled this variety at heirloom orchards.

Red Delicious

Truly delicious when it was named by Stark Brothers nurseries of Missouri in the late nineteenth century, this epitome of the supermarket apple has lost its appeal through years of selective breeding for looks rather than flavour. Uniformly red and thick-skinned, it lacks a crisp texture and the proper blend of sweet and tart. 'Merely sweet,' the British pomologist Edward Bunyard wryly observed in *The Anatomy of Dessert* (1929), 'is as nauseous as in human-kind.'

Reine de Reinette

This queen of the reinettes is accorded royal acclaim in France for its complex flavours. It has also been widely grown in England since Victorian times, although its title somehow switched genders there to become the 'King of the Pippins'. It has a gentle crunch and a citrus aftertaste, making it a treat both for eating fresh and for use in cooking.

Rhode Island Greening

One of the oldest and most popular commercial apples grown in America, this variety was famous for more than two centuries after it was discovered, supposedly growing outside a tavern in Green's End, Rhode Island, in 1650. But its name might also come from its green skin and greenish-white flesh. Known as an excellent apple for pies and all-round cooking, it is an heirloom alternative to the green Granny Smith.

Ribston Pippin

First grown in 1708 at Ribston Hall in Yorkshire, this variety became one of the most popular dessert apples in Victorian times. Yellow to green with red striations, it has creamy yellow flesh that some say tastes of pear. The first pips (seeds) came from Normandy, but the Ribston Pippin became a thoroughly English apple and may have been a parent of the famous English variety Cox's Orange Pippin.

Rome

Originating in Rome Township, Ohio, in the 1820s, this variety was long known as the queen of the baking apples. Bright red, crunchy and mildly tart, it is rarely mealy and holds its shape during baking.

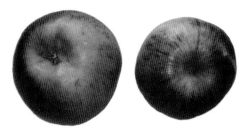

Ribston Pippin.

Rome.

Also known as Rome Beauty, it has a combination that is all too rare today, being both picture-perfect and tasty.

Sheep's Nose (also known as Black Gilliflower)

The gilliflower name refers to the clove-like aroma of this apple, a fragrance that people either love or hate. The sheep's nose appellation comes from its shape, tapering towards the base. This New England variety from the early 1800s has rich flavours that are particularly suited to cooking.

Snapdragon

This is Honeycrisp's latest offspring, released in 2013 by Cornell University in Geneva, New York, which has bred some of the most popular apples in today's market. Cornell promises that its latest creation will have Honeycrisp's juicy crispness and an even longer shelf life. Snapdragon, along with another new Cornell cultivar, RubyFrost, was released under an exclusive licensing agreement to a select group of growers, the marketing strategy employed by breeders today to ensure quality and maximum revenue.

Winecrisp

The name suggests the two qualities the breeders of this variety wanted to convey – a dark red colour and good crunch. But it has a third quality, a gene for resistance to apple scab, the greatest threat to apple crops and a disease that growers spray 15 to 20 times a season to prevent. It took twenty years for breeders from three American Midwestern universities to develop Winecrisp, which was finally released in 2009. It recalls an older, unrelated variety, Winesap, a popular heirloom from the nineteenth century overcome by twentieth-century technology.

Stayman Winesap.

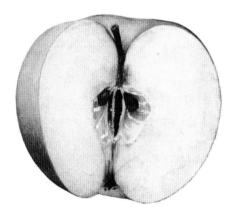

Winter Banana.

Winter Banana

An apple called 'banana' seems to be a contradiction in terms, but this variety's select followers attest to its banana aroma. Some reports say that it came to America with Dutch settlers, but its first record in the USA was in 1876 on a farm in Indiana. Its attractive colouring – a red blush over waxy yellow skin – made it a fancy fruit, sent abroad to wealthy English customers. Today the trees, which bear a profusion of blossoms, are largely used as orchard pollinators.

Worcester Pearmain.

Worcester Pearmain

Raised in the West Midlands, this pear-shaped dessert apple was introduced in 1874 and the following year earned a First Class Certificate from the Royal Horticultural Society. It has dark red skin stippled with white dots over a yellow background, and a pronounced strawberry flavour when fully ripe.

Zestar

Breeders of this apple were so enthusiastic that they included an exclamation point in its trademarked name, Zestar! This early-ripening apple, ready in August or September, was bred at the University of Minnesota to avoid harsh weather in that region's autumn season. Released in 1998, it followed the university's release of Honeycrisp in 1991. Together, Zestar and Honeycrisp became the parents of SweeTango (2010), the variety said to have a super crunch.

Timeline

Prehistory	Primitive shrubs of the rose family migrate from North America to Asia; birds disperse their seeds, dropping some on to the Tian Shan Mountains, where they survive the Ice Age and evolve into the progenitors of today's apple trees
c. 2600 BC	Apples buried in Sumerian tomb of Queen Puabi, a sign of their high value
c. 580–529 BC	Apple horticulture thrives in the Persian Empire of Cyrus the Great
c. 334 BC	Alexander the Great conquers Persia and brings apple horticulture to Greece
c. 120 BC–AD 1200	Traders on the Silk Road between China and Europe pick apples along their journeys through the Tian Shan mountain range, spreading the fruit to many countries
c. 27 BC–AD 300	Romans perfect apple grafting and cultivation, and spread it throughout their empire
c. 600–900	Muslims in the Middle East and Spain preserve and advance Roman apple growing
1066	Normans invade Britain, introducing new apple varieties and cider-making techniques

c. 1100	Cistercian monks begin to spread apple horticulture through their abbey orchards in Scotland, Germany, Sweden, Portugal and the eastern Mediterranean
1517	Following Martin Luther's challenge to Catholicism, Protestants spread throughout northern Europe and plant apple orchards, a crop suitable both to the climate and to their ethic of hard work
c. 1620s	European colonists begin to travel to North America, bringing apple seeds, grafts and seedlings to the New World
1621	The first shipment of European honeybees, essential pollinators of apple orchards, arrives in the English colony of Jamestown, Virginia
1654	Dutch colonists bring apples to South Africa and make fruit growing a requirement for settlers
1676	John Worlidge publishes a comprehensive treatise on British apples, evaluating them for the best cider
1788	English sea captains bring apples to Australia
1790	The British horticulturalist Thomas Andrew Knight conducts the first controlled programme of apple cross-breeding
1793	The German-Russian botanist Johann Sievers discovers *Malus sieversii* in the Tian Shan Mountains. It is later determined to be the ancestor of today's apples
c. 1800–1900	Horticultural and agricultural discoveries lead to an explosive time for apple production in Britain, Europe and America
c. 1806	John Chapman, soon to be known as Johnny Appleseed, begins a lifetime of planting apple seeds on the Midwestern American frontier
1809	The young Mary Ann Brailsford plants a seedling in her Nottinghamshire garden that bears fruit destined to become Bramley's Seedling, England's most famous cooking apple

1864	The influential preacher Henry Ward Beecher proclaims the apple America's 'true democratic fruit'
c. 1860s	The Temperance Movement against the sale of all alcoholic beverages, including cider, soars to new heights of activity in the USA, leading to the abandonment and destruction of many apple orchards
1872	The first refrigerated rail car begins operation, making it possible to transport apples and other perishable foods over long distances
c. 1880s–1900	American apple growers begin widespread use of pesticide sprays
1884	Robert Hogg publishes *The Fruit Manual: A Guide to the Fruits and Fruit Trees of Great Britain*, a highly detailed account that will become the standard reference for old English apple varieties
1894	Clarence Stark of Stark Brothers nursery in Missouri purchases the rights to growing an apple he later renames Red Delicious
1904	At the World's Fair in St Louis, fruit specialist J. T. Stinson proclaims 'an apple a day keeps the doctor away', a slogan that begins to transform the apple's image from the basis of an alcoholic drink to a healthy food
1914	Stark purchases the rights to propagating the apple he calls Golden Delicious
1920	Prohibition begins in the USA, outlawing the production and sale of alcoholic beverages, including fermented cider
c. 1920s	Growers in Washington State plant vast orchards of Red Delicious and Golden Delicious apples and begin promoting them in widespread marketing campaigns that overcome regional varieties

1929	Nikolai Vavilov, a Russian plant geneticist, finds forests of *Malus sieversii* in Kazakhstan and proclaims the variety the ancestor of today's apples
1942	Vavilov, arrested by the Soviet regime, dies in a Leningrad prison
c. 1946	British scientists develop controlled atmosphere techniques, allowing apples to be stored in warehouses without ripening for long periods of time
c. 1980s	Western horticulturalists visit Kazakhstan and bring back thousands of apple samples to study and preserve for genetic diversity
1989	An exposé of Alar, a chemical used on apples, leads to controversy and greater public awareness of pesticides
c. 1990s	China begins to take the lead in worldwide apple production
c. 1990s	The production of heirloom and organic apples and artisanal ciders increases rapidly and gains support as alternatives to the mass market
2006	The Honeycrisp (Honeycrunch) apple is declared the 'iPod of apples' for its astonishing market success
2010	An international group of plant geneticists sequences the genome of the apple, offering infinite possibilities for future apple cultivation

References

Introduction: Backyard Apples

1   Eric Sloane, *A Reverence for Wood* (New York, 1965), p. 84.
2   Jo Robinson, *Eating on the Wild Side: The Missing Link to Optimum Health* (New York, 2013), p. 7.
3   Sara Sciammacco, Environmental Working Group, 'Apples Top EWG's Dirty Dozen', 22 April 2013, at www.ewg.org.
4   Slow Food USA, Ark of Taste, 'Newtown Pippin Apple', at www.slowfoodusa.org, accessed 15 January 2014.
5   Ibid. Slow Food USA sponsors the programme of planting Newtown Pippins in New York City
6   Andrea Wulf, *The Brother Gardeners: Botany, Empire and the Birth of an Obsession* (London, 2008), p. 12.
7   Frank Browning, *Apples* (New York, 1998), p. 4.

1 Out of the Wild: An Ode and a Lament

1   All quotations in this chapter are from Henry David Thoreau, 'Wild Apples', *Atlantic Monthly*, November 1862, at www.theatlantic.com.

2 A Rose is a Rose is a Rose . . . is an Apple

1   Frank Browning, *Apples* (New York, 1998), p. 90.
2   Ibid.
3   Roger Yepsen, *Apples* (New York, 1994), p. 12.
4   Barrie E. Juniper and David J. Mabberley, *The Story of the Apple* (Portland, OR, 2006), p. 89.
5   Henry David Thoreau, 'Wild Apples', *Atlantic Monthly*, November 1862, at www.theatlantic.com.
6   Based on the genetic sequencing of the Golden Delicious apple in 2010, at www.biotechlearn.org.nz, accessed 26 September 2013.
7   Harold McGee, *On Food and Cooking: The Science and Lore of the Kitchen* (New York, 2004), p. 354.

8 Juniper and Mabberley, *The Story of the Apple*, p. 87.

9 Conversation with Ezekiel Goodband, orchardist, Scott Farm, Dummerston, Vermont, 5 September 2013.

10 Jo Robinson, *Eating on the Wild Side: The Missing Link to Optimum Health* (New York, 2013), p. 227.

11 Browning, *Apples*, p. 12.

12 Eric Sloane, *A Reverence for Wood* (New York, 1965), pp. 85, 81.

13 Association of University Technology Managers, The Better World Project, at www.betterworldproject.org, accessed 27 March 2013.

14 Robinson, *Eating on the Wild Side*, p. 228.

15 University of California, Center for Landscape and Urban Horticulture, 'Low Chill Apples', at www.ucanr.org, accessed 26 March 2013.

16 McGee, *On Food and Cooking*, p. 356.

17 Association of University Technology Managers, The Better World Project.

18 Rachel Hutton, 'With Honeycrisp's Patent Expiring, U of M Looks for New Apple', 1 October 2008, at www.citypages.com.

19 John Seabrook, 'Crunch: Building a Better Apple', *New Yorker*, 21 November 2011, p. 54.

20 Hutton, 'With Honeycrisp's Patent Expiring'.

21 American Society for Horticultural Science, 'Computerized Tool Takes a Bite out of Traditional Apple Testing', 13 December 2011, at www.sciencedaily.com.

22 Quoted in William Ellery Jones, ed., *Johnny Appleseed: A Voice in the Wilderness* (West Chester, PA, 2000), p. 35.

23 Child was also an abolitionist and women's rights activist, and is best known today for her American Thanksgiving poem 'Over the River and Through the Wood'.

24 Juniper and Mabberley, *The Story of the Apple*, p. 28.

25 Browning, *Apples*, p. 90.

26 Conversation with Carl Schwartz, U.S. Fish and Wildlife Service, New York Field Office, 18 March 2013.

27 Juniper and Mabberley, *The Story of the Apple*, p. 75.

28 Thoreau, 'Wild Apples'.

29 David Buchanan, *Taste, Memory: Forgotten Foods, Lost Flavors, and Why They Matter* (White River Junction, VT, 2012), p. 174.

30 Harold McGee, 'Stalking the Placid Apple's Untamed Kin', *New York Times*, 21 November 2007.

31 Juniper and Mabberley, *The Story of the Apple*, p. 91.

32 Ibid., p. 100.

33 Conversation with Ezekiel Goodband.

34 Juniper and Mabberley, *The Story of the Apple*, pp. 108–10.

35 Ibid., p. 113.

36 S. A. Beach, *The Apples of New York*, vol. 1 (Albany, NY, 1905), p. 13.

37 Ibid., p. 15.

38 Verlyn Klinkenborg, 'Apples, Apples, Apples', *New York Times*, 5 November 2009.

39 See www.theenglishappleman.com, accessed 24 March 2013.
40 'Crab Apple Trees: Long-term Apple Scab Resistance Remains Elusive, Expert Says', Purdue University *Horticulture*, 8 September 2009, at www.sciencedaily.com.

3 The Search for Sweetness

1 Henry David Thoreau, 'Wild Apples', *Atlantic Monthly*, November 1862, at www.theatlantic.com.
2 Barrie E. Juniper and David J. Mabberley, *The Story of the Apple* (Portland, OR, 2006), p. 87.
3 Ibid., pp. 17–22; Frank Browning, *Apples* (New York, 1998), p. 89.
4 Browning, *Apples*, p. 44.
5 Phillip L. Forsline, horticulturalist, U.S. Department of Agriculture's Plant Genetic Resources Unit, Geneva, New York, quoted in Michael Pollan, *The Botany of Desire* (New York, 2001), p. 54.
6 Juniper and Mabberley, *The Story of the Apple*, pp. 33, 181.
7 Ibid., p. 78.
8 Ibid., p. 93.
9 Andrew Dalby, *Food in the Ancient World from A to Z* (London, 2013), p. 19.
10 Juniper and Mabberley, *The Story of the Apple*, p. 90.
11 John M. Wilkins and Shaun Hill, *Food in the Ancient World* (Malden, MA, and Oxford, 2006), p. 47.
12 Wilhelmina Feemster Jashemski and Frederick G. Meyer, *The Natural History of Pompeii* (Cambridge, 2002), pp. 124–5.
13 Juniper and Mabberley, *The Story of the Apple*, p. 129.
14 Ibid., p. 131.
15 Erika Janik, 'How the Apple Took Over the Planet', in *Apple: A Global History* (London, 2011), excerpt at www.salon.com, 25 October 2011.
16 Joan Morgan and Alison Richards, *The Book of Apples* (London, 1993), p. 56.
17 Marcus Woodward, ed., *Leaves from Gerard's Herball* (New York, 1969), p. 93.
18 Morgan and Richards, *The Book of Apples*, pp. 60–61.
19 Janik, 'How the Apple Took Over the Planet'.
20 Ezekiel Goodband, blog entry, July 2013, at www.scottfarmvermont.org.
21 Tim Hensley, 'A Curious Tale: The Apple in North America', Brooklyn Botanic Garden online, 2 June 2005, at www.bbg.org.
22 Morgan and Richards, *The Book of Apples*, p. 110.
23 Pollan, *The Botany of Desire*, p. 51.

4 Cider Chronicles

1 Henry David Thoreau, 'Wild Apples', *Atlantic Monthly*, November 1862, at www.theatlantic.com.
2 Frank Browning, *Apples* (New York, 1998), p. 168.
3 Joan Morgan and Alison Richards, *The Book of Apples* (London, 1993), p. 57.

4 Ibid.

5 Marcus Woodward, ed., *Leaves from Gerard's Herball* (New York, 1969), p. 92.

6 Ibid., p. 94.

7 Browning, *Apples*, p. 170.

8 Morgan and Richards, *The Book of Apples*, p. 145; other sources report cider being used as wages in Somerset until the Second World War.

9 Tom Burford, *The Apples of North America* (Portland, OR, 2013), p. 12.

10 William Kerrigan, *Johnny Appleseed and the American Orchard* (Baltimore, MD, 2012), p. 145.

11 Ron Chernow, *Titan: The Life of John D. Rockefeller, Sr.* (New York, 2004), p. 191.

12 Thoreau, 'Wild Apples'.

13 Kerrigan, *Johnny Appleseed*, p. 147.

14 Morgan and Richards, *The Book of Apples*, p. 126.

15 See www.hardciderinternational.com, accessed 18 February 2013.

16 Morgan and Richards, *The Book of Apples*, p. 144.

17 David Buchanan, *Taste, Memory: Forgotten Foods, Lost Flavors, and Why They Matter* (White River Junction, VT, 2012), p. 193.

18 See www.camra.org.uk/aboutcider, accessed 6 January 2014.

19 Adam Minter, 'Coming Your Way: China's Rotten Apples', 30 September 2013, at www.bloombergview.com.

20 Jennifer Ladonne, 'Sophisticated Cider', *France Today*, 17 June 2010, at www.francetoday.com.

21 'Forgotten Fruit Manifesto', at www.slowfoodusa.org, accessed 29 March 2013.

22 Buchanan, *Taste, Memory*, pp. 205–6.

23 See www.origsin.com, accessed 3 March 2013.

24 'Bulmers at its Best', www.bbc.co.uk/herefordandworcester, accessed 14 November 2013.

25 Pete Brown, 'Cider Around the World', 24 February 2012, at www.theguardian.com.

26 Warren Schultz, 'A Brew of Their Own', *Gourmet*, March 2006, p. 144.

27 Tess Jewell-Larsen, 'Cider in Mexico Shouldn't Just be for Christmas: Q&A with Sidra Sierra Norte', 20 September 2012, at www.hardciderinternational.com.

28 Andrew Knowlton, 'Hard Cider, Huge Market', *Bon Appétit*, 21 May 2013, at www.bonappetit.com.

29 Ibid.

5 The American Apple

1 Joan Morgan and Alison Richards, *The Book of Apples* (London, 1993), p. 66.

2 Tammy Horn, *Bees in America* (Lexington, KY, 2006), p. 21.

3 Tom Turpin, 'Honey Bees not Native to North America', Purdue University News, 11 November 1999, at www.agriculture.purdue.edu.

4 Charles Louis Flint et al., *One Hundred Years' Progress of the United States* (Hartford, CT, 1871), cited in Bruce Weber, *The Apple of America: The Apple in 19th Century American Art*, exh. cat., Berry Hill Galleries, New York (1993), p. 14.

5 Andrea Wulf, *The Brother Gardeners: Botany, Empire and the Birth of an Obsession* (London, 2008), p. 5.

6 'The Newtown Pippin (Albemarle): A History Published 110 Years Ago', 15 March 2012, at www.heirloomorchardist.com.

7 From 'Johnny Appleseed', by Florence Boyce Davis, in William Ellery Jones, ed., *Johnny Appleseed: A Voice in the Wilderness* (West Chester, PA, 2000), p. 50.

8 California Department of Finance, at www.ca.gov, accessed 18 February 2013.

9 Elise Warner, 'The Apple, "Our Democratic Fruit"', *American Spirit*, vol. CXLVII, September/October 2013, p. 28.

10 William Kerrigan, *Johnny Appleseed and the American Orchard* (Baltimore, MD, 2012), p. 4.

11 Robert Price, 'Johnny Appleseed in American Folklore and Literature', in Jones, *Johnny Appleseed*, p. 26.

12 Jones, *Johnny Appleseed*, p. 99.

13 Kerrigan, *Johnny Appleseed*, p. 88.

14 Michael Pollan, *The Botany of Desire* (New York, 2001), pp. 9, 39.

15 Kerrigan, *Johnny Appleseed*, p. 173.

16 S. A. Beach, *The Apples of New York*, vol. 1 (Albany, NY, 1905), pp. 5–6.

17 Tom Brown, 'Man Keeps History Alive with Junaluska Apple Find', *Blue Ridge Times-News*, 17 January 2011, at www.blueridgenow.com.

18 Kerrigan, *Johnny Appleseed*, p. 68.

19 Ibid., pp. 91–3.

20 Ibid., p. 74.

21 Bruce Weber, *The Apple of America: The Apple in 19th Century American Art*, exh. cat., Berry Hill Galleries, New York (1993), p. 10.

22 Ibid.

23 Ibid.

24 Louisa May Alcott, *Transcendental Wild Oats* (Boston, MA, 1873), pp. 51–2.

25 John Matteson, *Eden's Outcasts: The Story of Louisa May Alcott and her Father* (New York, 2007), p. 141.

26 Ibid., p. 148.

27 Alcott, *Transcendental Wild Oats*, pp. 28–9.

28 Ibid., p. 62.

29 Ron Chernow, *Titan: The Life of John D. Rockefeller, Sr.* (New York, 2004), p. 222.

30 Morgan and Richards, *The Book of Apples*, p. 71.

31 Weber, *The Apple of America*, p. 19.

32 Henry James, *The American Scene* [London, 1907] (New York, 1968), p. 67.

33 Ibid., p. 170.

34 'Modern Nature: Georgia O'Keeffe and Lake George', exhibition at the
    Hyde Collection, Glens Fall, New York, 15 June–15 September 2013.
35 Elizabeth Hutton Turner, *Georgia O'Keeffe: The Poetry of Things* (New Haven,
    CT, 1999), p. 1.
36 Ibid., p. 53.
37 Quoted in Sarah E. Greenough, 'From the American Earth: Alfred
    Stieglitz's Photographs of Apples', *Art Journal*, Spring 1981, p. 49.
38 Quoted in ibid., p. 48.
39 Quoted in ibid.
40 Permanent exhibition at Robert Frost Stone House Museum, Shaftsbury,
    Vermont, visited 9 October 2013.
41 Ibid.
42 Ibid.
43 Beach, *The Apples of New York*, p. 7.
44 Jules Janick et al., 'Apples', *Horticultural Review*, Purdue University, 1996,
    p. 6, at www.hort.purdue.edu.
45 Anne Raver, 'He Keeps Ancient Apples Fresh and Crisp', *New York Times*,
    2 March 2011.

6 Apple Adulation

1 See www.westminster-abbey.org, accessed 23 October 2013.
2 Barrie E. Juniper and David J. Mabberley, *The Story of the Apple* (Portland,
   OR, 2006), p. 133.
3 Quoted in William Kerrigan, *Johnny Appleseed and the American Orchard*
   (Baltimore, MD, 2012), p. 74.
4 Joan Morgan and Alison Richards, *The Book of Apples* (London, 1993),
   p. 64.
5 Ibid., p. 65.
6 Ibid., p. 89.
7 Edward Bunyard, *The Epicure's Companion* (London, 1937), p. 156, quoted in
   Morgan and Richards, *The Book of Apples*, p. 88.
8 Tim Hensley, 'A Curious Tale: The Apple in North America', Brooklyn
   Botanic Garden online, 2 June 2005, at www.bbg.org.
9 Anya von Bremzen, *Mastering the Art of Soviet Cooking: A Memoir of Food and
   Longing* (New York, 2013), p. 34.
10 George Bunyard, *Fruit Farming for Profit* (Maidstone, 1881), quoted in
   Morgan and Richards, *The Book of Apples*, p. 112.
11 *Journal of Horticulture and Cottage Gardener*, vol. XXI, 1890, quoted in Morgan
   and Richards, *The Book of Apples*, p. 91.
12 See www.englishapplesandpears.co.uk, accessed 21 March 2013.
13 Edward Bunyard, *The Anatomy of Dessert* (London, 1929), pp. 3, 12.
14 Bruce Weber, *The Apple of America: The Apple in 19th Century American Art*, exh.
   cat., Berry Hill Galleries, New York (1993), p. 15.
15 Henry David Thoreau, 'Wild Apples', *Atlantic Monthly*, November 1862, at
   www.theatlantic.com.

16 C. J. Bulliet, *Apples and Madonnas: Emotional Expression in Modern Art* (New York, 1930), p. 4.

17 Meyer Schapiro, *Paul Cézanne* (New York, 1988), p. 96.

18 Deborah Rieselman, 'Photography Professor Researches Japanese Method of Raising Apples', *University of Cincinnati Magazine*, April 2008, at http://magazine.uc.edu.

19 Quoted in Penelope Hobhouse, *Plants in Garden History* (London, 1997), p. 65.

20 John Ruskin, 'Notes on Some of the Principal Pictures Exhibited in the Rooms of the Royal Academy, etc.', in E. T. Cook and John Wedderburn, eds, *The Complete Works of John Ruskin* (London, 1903–12), quoted in Weber, *The Apple of America*, p. 10.

21 Quoted in Weber, *The Apple of America*, p. 10.

22 Quoted in ibid.

23 Michael A. Dirr, *Dirr's Hardy Trees and Shrubs: An Illustrated Encyclopedia* (Portland, OR, 1997), p. 248.

24 S. A. Beach, *The Apples of New York* (Albany, NY, 1905), vol. I, p. 8.

25 Morgan and Richards, *The Book of Apples*, p. 93.

26 Eric Sloane, *A Reverence for Wood* (New York, 1965), p. 41.

27 Andy Dolan, 'Sir Isaac Newton's Apple Tree Falls Victim . . . after Visitors Damage its Roots', 12 May 2011, at www.dailymail.co.uk.

28 Ajai Shukla, 'Isaac Newton's Apple Tree Travels in Space Shuttle Atlantis', 16 May 2010, at www.business-standard.com.

29 See www.bramleyapples.co.uk, accessed 1 March 2013.

30 Larz F. Neilson, 'Wilmington: The Home of the Baldwin Apple', at http://homenewshere.com, accessed 21 October 2013.

31 Morgan and Richards, *The Book of Apples*, p. 146.

32 Henry S. Burrage, *Baptist Hymn Writers and Their Hymns* (Portland, ME, 1888).

33 Conversation with Carl Schwartz, U.S. Fish and Wildlife Service, New York Field Office, 18 March 2013.

7 Good Apples

1 Frank Browning, *Apples* (New York, 1998), p. 86.

2 Abbie Farwell Brown, 'The King's Pie', *St Nicholas Magazine*, 1911.

3 Andrew Dalby, *Food in the Ancient World from A to Z* (London, 2013), p. 19.

4 William Kerrigan, *Johnny Appleseed and the American Orchard* (Baltimore, MD, 2012), p. 187.

5 T. Colin Campbell, *Whole: Rethinking the Science of Nutrition* (Dallas, TX, 2013), p. 154.

6 Jo Robinson, *Eating on the Wild Side: The Missing Link to Optimum Health* (New York, 2013), p. 228.

7 Ibid., p. 217.

8 Ibid., p. 226.

9 Ibid., p. 225. The tests were performed in 2006 by the French National Institute for Health and Medical Research.

10 Commonwealth Science and Industrial Research Organization Australia, 6 December 2006, at www.sciencedaily.com.
11 Robinson, *Eating on the Wild Side*, p. 226.
12 Tara Parker-Pope, 'New Evidence for an Apple-a-Day', *New York Times*, 15 September 2011.
13 Browning, *Apples*, p. 139.
14 Conversation with Ezekiel Goodband, orchardist, Scott Farm, Dummerston, Vermont, 5 September 2013.
15 Robinson, *Eating on the Wild Side*, p. 227.
16 Jennifer Lee, 'Should the Big Apple's Official Apple be Green?', *New York Times*, 24 April 2009, at http://cityroom.blogs.nytimes.com.

8 Bad Apples

1 Henry David Thoreau, 'Wild Apples', *Atlantic Monthly*, November 1862, at www.theatlantic.com.
2 Ernst and Johanna Lehner, *Folklore and Symbolism of Flowers, Plants and Trees* (Mineola, NY, 2003), p. 19.
3 The print, by Theodor de Bry, appears in Thomas Hariot, *A Brief and True Report of the New Found Land of Virginia* (London, 1590).
4 See notes on Cranach's painting of the Judgement of Paris from the Victoria and Albert Museum, at www.collections.vam.ac.uk, accessed 14 December 2013.
5 Thoreau, 'Wild Apples'.
6 Ibid.
7 Debra Mancoff, *The Garden in Art* (London, 2011), p. 86.
8 Meyer Schapiro, 'The Apples of Cézanne', in *Modern Art 19th and 20th Centuries: Selected Papers* (New York, 1968), p. 5.
9 Ibid., pp. 5–6.
10 Dora Jane Hamblin, 'Has the Garden of Eden been Located at Last?', *Smithsonian* magazine, vol. XVIII, no. 2, May 1987, pp. 127–35.
11 John Matteson, *Eden's Outcasts: The Story of Louisa May Alcott and her Father* (New York, 2007), p. 72.
12 See www.barrypopik.com, accessed 16 January 2014.
13 Frank Bruni, 'The Siren and the Spook', *New York Times*, 12 November 2012.
14 Barrie E. Juniper and David J. Mabberley, *The Story of the Apple* (Portland, OR, 2006), p. 104.
15 Andrea Wulf, *The Brother Gardeners: Botany, Empire and the Birth of an Obsession* (London, 2008), pp. 7, 11.
16 Frank Browning, *Apples* (New York, 1998), p. 11.
17 Ibid., p. 77.
18 Andrew Dalby, *Food in the Ancient World from A to Z* (London, 2013), p. 19.
19 Quoted in Wilhelmina Feemster Jashemski and Frederick G. Meyer, *The Natural History of Pompeii* (Cambridge, 2002), p. 125.
20 See www.vangoghvodka.com, accessed 16 January 2014.
21 Roger Yepsen, *Apples* (New York, 1994), p. 14.

22 Browning, *Apples*, p. 24.

23 William Kerrigan, *Johnny Appleseed and the American Orchard* (Baltimore, MD, 2012), p. 175.

24 Andrea Rock, 'Debate Grows over Arsenic in Apple Juice', *Consumer Reports*, 14 September 2011, at www.consumerreports.org.

25 Browning, *Apples*, p. 38.

26 Alan Garner, 'My Hero: Alan Turing', *The Guardian*, 11 November 2011, at www.theguardian.com.

27 See www.asrcreviews.org, accessed 16 January 2013; Michael Moss, *Salt, Sugar, Fat: How the Food Giants Hooked Us* (New York, 2013), pp. 87–9.

28 Moss, *Salt, Sugar, Fat*, pp. 88–9.

9 Misplaced Apples

1 Barrie E. Juniper and David J. Mabberley, *The Story of the Apple* (Portland, OR, 2006), pp. 89–90.

2 Dora Jane Hamblin, 'Has the Garden of Eden been Located at Last?', *Smithsonian* magazine, vol. XVIII, no. 2, May 1987, pp. 127–35.

3 Dan Koeppel, *Banana: The Fate of the Fruit that Changed the World* (New York, 2008), p. 6.

4 Ibid., p. 7.

5 Andrew Dalby, *Food in the Ancient World from A to Z* (London, 2013), p. 19.

6 Quoted in Bonnie Rosenstock, 'Peter's Pear Tree Plaque is Going Home at Long Last', *The Villager*, vol. LXXIV, no. 45, 16–22 March 2005, at http://thevillager.com.

7 New-York Historical Society Museum and Library at www.nyhistory.org, accessed 13 September 2013.

8 Marcus Woodward, ed., *Leaves from Gerard's Herball* (New York, 1985), p. 81.

9 Ibid., p. 79.

10 Ernst and Johanna Lehner, *Folklore and Symbolism of Flowers, Plants and Trees* (Mineola, NY, 2003), p. 85.

11 'Red Delicious or Wolf Apple? Brazilian Savanna Fruits High in Antioxidants', *Science Daily*, 22 August 2013, at www.sciencedaily.com.

12 Andrew Graham-Dixon, '*Le Jeu de Morre* by René Magritte, 1966; The Apple Corp. Logo, 1967', *Sunday Telegraph*, 3 September 2000, at www.andrewgrahamdixon.com.

13 Andrea Elliott, 'Jef Raskin, 61, Developer of Apple Macintosh, is Dead', *New York Times*, 28 February 2005, at www.nytimes.com.

10 The Politics of Pomology

1 Eleanor Atkinson, *The Romance of the Sower* (New York, 1915), foreword. Atkinson also wrote an early and sentimental book about one of the best-known dog stories, *Greyfriars Bobby* (1912).

2 William Kerrigan, *Johnny Appleseed and the American Orchard* (Baltimore, MD, 2012), p. 148.

3 Sara Calian, 'Urban Scrumpers Are Picking the Forbidden Fruit', *Wall Street Journal*, 29 October 2010, at http://online.wsj.com.

4 Kerrigan, *Johnny Appleseed*, pp. 161–7.

5 Ibid., pp. 66–7.

6 Daniel Okrent, *Great Fortune: The Epic of Rockefeller Center* (New York, 2004), p. 188.

7 James McWilliams, 'Depression Apples', 17 February 2010, at www.freakonomics.com.

8 Kerrigan, *Johnny Appleseed*, pp. 158–9.

9 Ibid., p. 179.

10 Quoted in David Buchanan, *Taste, Memory: Forgotten Foods, Lost Flavors, and Why They Matter* (White River Junction, VT, 2012), p. 60.

11 Kerrigan, *Johnny Appleseed*, p. 186.

12 Ibid., p. 185.

13 Maria Anne Boerngen, *Trade and Welfare Effects of Japan's Revised Import Protocol for American Apples,* thesis, University of Illinois at Urbana-Champaign (2008) (Ann Arbor, MI, 2008), pp. 2–6.

14 Barrie E. Juniper and David J. Mabberley, *The Story of the Apple* (Portland, OR, 2006), p. 105.

15 Kerrigan, *Johnny Appleseed*, p. 175.

16 John B. Oakes, 'A Silent Spring, for Kids', 'Opinion' page, *New York Times*, 30 March 1989.

17 Kerrigan, *Johnny Appleseed*, p. 185.

18 Mitch Lynd, 'Great Moments in Apple History', Midwest Apple Improvement Association, at www.hort.purdue.edu, accessed 11 November 2012.

19 S. A. Beach, *The Apples of New York* (Albany, NY, 1905), vol. I, p. 5.

20 Frank Browning, *Apples* (New York, 1998), pp. 50–2. Browning visited Djangaliev in Kazakhstan in 1992.

21 Calian, 'Urban Scrumpers are Picking the Forbidden Fruit'.

11 Apples Today and Tomorrow

1 See www.fruit-crops.com, Chapter IV, Production, accessed 17 January 2013.

2 See www.groworganicapples.com, accessed 24 March 2013.

3 Radio interview with Elizabeth Ryan, Breezy Hill Orchards, on WNYC, Leonard Lopate Show, 27 September 2013.

4 Conversation with Ezekiel Goodband, orchardist, Scott Farm, Dummerston, Vermont, 5 September 2013.

5 Ibid.

6 Ibid.

7 Quoted in Anne Raver, 'Totally Green Apples', *New York Times*, 16 November 2011, at www.nytimes.com.

8 Ibid.

9 'Apples: Fruit of Knowledge', *Martha Stewart Living*, October 2012, p. 119; available online at www.marthastewart.com.

10 See www.scottfarmvermont.com, accessed 18 September 2013.

11 Anne Raver, 'He Keeps Ancient Apples Fresh and Crisp', *New York Times*, 2 March 2011.

12 See www.kuffelcreek.com, accessed 17 January 2014.

13 Conversation with Ezekiel Goodband.

14 David Buchanan, *Taste, Memory: Forgotten Foods, Lost Flavors, and Why They Matter* (White River Junction, VT, 2012), pp. 62–3.

15 See www.theenglishappleman.com, accessed 24 March 2013.

16 Harold McGee, 'Stalking the Placid Apple's Untamed Kin', *New York Times*, 21 November 2007.

17 'Crab Apple Trees: Long-term Apple Scab Resistance Remains Elusive, Expert Says', Purdue University *Horticulture*, 8 September 2009, at www.sciencedaily.com.

18 Quoted in Rachel Hutton, 'With Honeycrisp's Patent Expiring, U of M Looks for New Apple', 1 October 2008, at www.citypages.com.

19 Jennifer Ackerman, 'Food: How Altered', *National Geographic*, at http://environment.nationalgeographic.com, accessed 14 September 2013.

20 Andrew Pollack, 'That Fresh Look, Genetically Buffed', *New York Times*, 12 July 2012.

21 John Seabrook, 'Crunch: Building a Better Apple', *New Yorker*, 21 November 2011, p. 2.

22 Ashlee Vance, 'Minnesota's Enormous Apples Computer', *New York Times*, 10 December 2009.

23 Melissa Block, interview with John Seabrook, 'All Things Considered', National Public Radio, 19 November 2011.

24 S. K. Brown and K. E. Maloney, 'Making Sense of New Apple Varieties, Trademarks and Clubs', New York State Agricultural Experiment Station, Cornell University, Geneva, New York, 16 September 2009, at www.nyshs.org.

25 Conversation with Jim Perry, Perry Orchards, White Creek, New York, 13 November 2013.

26 Lizette Alvarez, 'Citrus Disease with no Cure is Ravaging Florida Groves', *New York Times*, 9 May 2013; Dan Koeppel, *Banana: The Fate of the Fruit that Changed the World* (New York, 2008), p. xviii.

27 Mitch Lynd, quoted in Frank Browning, *Apples* (New York, 1998), p. 210.

Select Bibliography

Alcott, Louisa May, *Transcendental Wild Oats* (Boston, MA, 1873)

Beach, S. A., *The Apples of New York* (Albany, NY, 1905)

Browning, Frank, *Apples* (New York, 1998)

Buchanan, David, *Taste, Memory: Forgotten Foods, Lost Flavors, and Why They Matter* (White River Junction, VT, 2012)

Bunyard, Edward, *The Anatomy of Dessert* (London, 1929)

Jones, William Ellery, ed., *Johnny Appleseed: A Voice in the Wilderness* (West Chester, PA, 2000)

Juniper, Barrie E., and David J. Mabberley, *The Story of the Apple* (Portland, OR, 2006)

Kerrigan, William, *Johnny Appleseed and the American Orchard* (Baltimore, MD, 2012)

Matteson, John, *Eden's Outcasts: The Story of Louisa May Alcott and her Father* (New York, 2007)

Morgan, Joan, and Alison Richards, *The Book of Apples* (London, 1993)

Pollan, Michael, *The Botany of Desire* (New York, 2001)

Robinson, Jo, *Eating on the Wild Side: The Missing Link to Optimum Health* (New York, 2013)

Weber, Bruce, *The Apple of America: The Apple in 19th Century American Art*, exh. cat., Berry Hill Galleries, New York (1993)

Wilkins, John M., and Shaun Hill, *Food in the Ancient World* (Malden, MA, and Oxford, 2006)

Wulf, Andrea, *The Brother Gardeners: Botany, Empire and the Birth of an Obsession* (London, 2008)

Yepsen, Roger, *Apples* (New York, 1994)

Associations and Websites

ADAM'S APPLES
Personal, informative reflections on apples, including an extensive
directory of commercial and heirloom varieties.
www.adamsapples.blogspot.com

AUSTRALIAN APPLES
Listings of Australian varieties, growers and recipes.
www.aussieapples.com

ECO APPLE PROGRAM
Information about Integrated Pest Management methods for apple growing.
www.redtomato.org/ecoapple.php

THE ENGLISH APPLE MAN
History of and information about English apple
growing from a third-generation orchardist.
www.theenglishappleman.com

ENGLISH APPLES & PEARS
An association of English growers promoting and
providing information about English varieties.
www.englishapplesandpears.co.uk

FALLEN FRUIT
A collaboration of activist artists promoting the planting
of fruit trees and the harvesting of fruit on public land.
www.fallenfruit.org

GROW ORGANIC APPLES: HOLISTIC ORCHARD NETWORK
Information about organic apple growing.
www.groworganicapples.com

A LIFE OF APPLES
Apple history and personal recollections from an American apple harvester.
www.appleharvester.blogspot.com

NATIONAL FRUIT COLLECTION
Database and photographs of one of the world's largest fruit collections.
www.nationalfruitcollection.org.uk

NEW YORK STATE AGRICULTURAL EXPERIMENT STATION
Breeder, in cooperation with Cornell University, of many of the most
popular apple cultivars, and the location of the U.S. Plant Genetic
Resources Unit, a vast preserve of apple germplasm.
www.nysaes.cornell.edu

ORANGE PIPPIN
Extensive listings of apple varieties and orchards,
primarily in North America and the UK.
www.orangepippin.com

SCOTT FARM
Seasonal tours and tastings of a 5,000-tree heirloom apple orchard
in Dummerston, Vermont, owned by Landmark Trust USA, adjacent
to the site of the historic home of Rudyard Kipling.
www.scottfarmvermont.com

SLOW FOOD MOVEMENT
Publications and programmes for finding, growing and
promoting heirloom apples in the USA and UK.
www.slowfoodusa.org
www.slowfood.org.uk

U.S. APPLE ASSOCIATION
Represents the U.S. apple industry, including information about government
affairs, apples and apple products.
www.usapple.org

Acknowledgements

Whenever friends and neighbours heard that I was writing a book about apples, everyone had something to share, a tribute to the universal appeal of apples. Thanks to all who loaned me books, articles and pictures or told me about other sources, nearly all of which ended up in this book in some form or other. I greatly appreciate the help enthusiastically provided by Sue Bastian, Gayle and Mick Fiato, Al and Debra Klein, Debra Mancoff, Lincoln and Margaret Miller and Nancy Clark Strauss. I am especially grateful to Barbara Villet, who not only loaned me her prized copy of the antique, two-volume *The Apples of New York* (which I kept for an unconscionably long period of time), but also took the time to have prints made from the book for my use here.

Ezekiel Goodband of the historic Scott Farm in Dummerston, Vermont, took time in the midst of his hectic fall harvest season to take me on a tasting tour of the extensive apple orchard that he created with his incredible variety of heirloom grafts. He also patiently shared his knowledge and experience, along with his wry sense of humour, helping me understand many mysteries of apple growing. Jim Perry of Perry Orchards in White Creek, New York, provided the perspective of a small apple grower, a valuable point of view reflecting that of countless small orchardists who continue, despite difficult pressures, to provide fresh apples and cider as an alternative to mass market fruit.

David Burns, Matias Viegener and Austin Young, the talented artists of the Fallen Fruit collaborative in Los Angeles, generously permitted the reproduction of their striking poster, 'Urban Fruit Action'. Margaret Roach, the creator of a unique garden and delightful website, 'A Way to Garden', kindly allowed me to use a photograph of her wonderfully craggy old apple tree, still bearing fruit after more than a century on a steep hillside in the Taconic Mountains of New York.

I wrote this book during a year of an amazing apple harvest in upstate New York – greater than any other in recent history, so everyone said. Surrounded by apples, I often thought of Marjorie Lutz who more than 40 years ago planted several crab apple and apple trees around her home, now my backyard. They have fed and delighted me and my husband, Charlie, along with flocks of robins and waxwings and generations of hungry deer and squirrels. Thanks also to Marjorie for allowing the ancient apple tree in our meadow to remain a thing of beauty. And thanks always to Charlie, who picks the apples with me, loves the apple sauce and keeps me going through all of my writing adventures.

Photo Acknowledgements

The author and publishers wish to express their thanks to the below sources of illustrative material and/or permission to reproduce it. (Some information not placed in the captions for reasons of brevity is also given below.)

Photo APAimages/Rex Features: p. 28; photos author: pp. 6, 8, 14, 38, 64, 89, 192, 205, 208 (middle), 222; photo BiltOn Graphics/BigstockPhoto: p. 189; photo © Jacques Boyer/Roger-Viollet/Rex Features: pp. 61, 75, 106; British Museum, London (photo © The Trustees of the British Museum): p. 57; photos © The Trustees of the British Museum, London: pp. 21, 42, 102, 122, 127, 139, 159; photo brookebecker/BigstockPhoto: p. 82; photo Paul Brown/Rex Features: pp. 97–8; photo dejavu/BigstockPhoto: p. 32; photo Evan-Amos: p. 29; photos Everett Collection/Rex Features: pp. 128, 168, 171; photo F1 Online/Rex Features: p. 138; photo Food and Drink/Rex Features: p. 200; Frans Hals Museum, Harlem: p. 92; photo Anthony Hammond/Rex Features: p. 197; photo I.B.L./Rex Features: p. 156; photo Image Broker/Rex Features: p. 165; photo Henryk T. Kaiser/Rex Features: p. 184; photo kimmyrm/BigstockPhoto: p. 70; Ross Kummer/BigstockPhoto: p. 72; Library of Congress, Washington, DC: pp. 18, 56 (top), 65, 108, 109, 119, 126 (top), 129 (foot), 130, 136, 149, 150, 174, 175, 176, 177; photo Magimix/Solent News/Rex Features: p. 164; Milwaukee Art Museum, Wisconsin: p. 94; photo Monkey Business Images/Rex Features: p. 78; Musée d'Orsay, Paris: p. 112; photo © Neurdein/Roger-Viollet/Rex Features 126 (foot), photo photohomepage/BigstockPhoto: p. 113; plantillustrations.org: pp. 20, 116, 196; from *The Pomological Magazine*, V/2 (1839): p. 55; private collections: pp. 12, 46; photo Quirky China News/Rex Features: pp. 186–7; photo radubalint/BigstockPhoto: p. 202; photo © Roger-Viollet/Rex Features: pp. 68, 71; photo Vicki Rosenzweig: p. 213; from *St Nicholas: An Illustrated Magazine for Young Folks*, XXXVIII (January 1911): p. 130; photo sarahdoow/BigstockPhoto: p. 16; photo songbird839/BigstockPhoto: p. 58 (foot); photo Pete Souza – White House via CNP/Rex Features: p. 79; Richard Sowersby/Rex Features: p. 74; Urban Fruit Action, Public Billboard Series, 2005, by Fallen Fruit Collaborative (David Burns, Matias Viegener and Austin Young): p. 183; photo U.S. National Library of Medicine (History of Medicine

Division), Bethesda, Maryland: pp. 132, 154; Victoria & Albert Museum, London (photos V&A Images): pp. 22, 49, 51, 52, 56 (foot), 58 (top), 62, 104, 114, 124, 125, 129 (top), 140, 162; Werner-Forman Archive: p. 46; photo WestEnd61/ Rex Features: p. 146; photo YURY TARANIK/iStock International: p. 24.

Index